TIM ATKINS

COLLECTED

PETRARCH

PETRARCH

COLLECTED

TIM ATKINS

MIMIH

David Kelly-Mancaux

PREFACE

Laird Hunt

INTRODUCTION

Jèssica Pujol i Duran

CRATER 2014

The world is a comedy to those that think; a tragedy to those that feel.

Horace Walpole

When you try to dig what really jumped with the great swingers of yesteryear, you can't really get straight with the history books. You got to be a reincarnation cat like myself; you've got to re-dig and re-call the ball

Lord Buckley

I cram my little works with another's words

Petrarch

Every problem to me is a problem of living. I make no attempt to translate.

Kenneth Patchen

He says

we say

she says

Gertrude Stein

Translation of Georges Hugnet's "Enfances"

PREFACE
BY LAIRD HUNT

& now I am here to tell you all that I have discovered
That living is one of the best things—there where I ripped it

Petrarch by Tim Atkins. One mind's field of words bent on/by another's.

Consider:

The Cervantine journey, which loops out and back, is half-imagined, half-remembered, half-exploded (yes, the mind's field; yes, that many halves). Loops out of nothing into something and something into nothing and back again and back. The Cervantine journey, which glories in particulars, revels in gleaming specificities, spews abstractions galore. Leaves in its wake an open archive of interleaved exigencies, hyperbolic intercessions.

Translation as the Cervantine journey. Translation as transformation. As pitched battle. As acknowledgement. As celebration. As poetry. As betrayal.

There is one thing and then there is another. It is our oldest story. It isn't even ours. Maybe that's the best part of it.

Petrarch by Tim Atkins as written by Miguel de Cervantes. Is a dream I had, though didn't know I was having, some 20 years ago when I met Tim in Eleni Sikelianos's kitchen in the Castro in San Francisco. He was a poet. From

England though not, or only partially, *of* England. He had already written and published a book but didn't want to talk about that book. He wanted to talk about Bernadette Mayer, Alice Notley, Ted Berrigan, Ron Padgett, Anne Waldman, Phil Whalen, Lew Welch, Carla Harryman, Frank O'Hara. He wanted to talk about Allen Ginsberg, Lewis Warsh, Gary Snyder, Joanne Kyger, Joe Ceravolo, Tom Raworth and Jean Follain. He wanted to talk about Charles Bernstein and Susan Howe and Barrett Watten and Bruce Andrews and Leslie Scalapino. He wanted to talk about art and music and football and the state of things in England. He was in Eleni Sikelianos's kitchen. They were pals. Sold.

Some time later, in the late '90s, we were in Fulham, waiting for our good friend Jonathan on Tim's roof. Jonathan was late, very late. It was perfect. Jonathan's lateness gave a shape to the books we talked about, to the drinks we drank, to the food we ate, to the cigarettes mostly I smoked. There were manuscripts by both of us downstairs. Tim was working on his sonnets. His sonnets that were responding to Mayer's sonnets, to Berrigan's, not to mention to everything he was reading or dying to read. His sonnets that were in the coming years to become instances of anticipatory plagiarism of his own *Petrarch*. *Petrarch* that exudes the sense that all of Tim's past and future (yes, I mean that) poetic concerns have been allowed to pour into it. It (*Petrarch*) is smart, sharp, erudite and easy-going. It is made out of many, many poems, so that it is somehow both quite short and very long. Petrarch is everywhere in its pages, but so are Lisa Jarnot and Eleni and Issa and Buson and Tu Fu. Poets he loved then and still loves and will keep on, one easily imagines, loving. Put otherwise: *Petrarch* was already there with us that day on Tim's roof in Fulham. There with us as we waited for Jonathan who did, to our delight, finally arrive. And in style. The drinking and smoking and talking continued. The three of us had an interest in the work of Stephen Rodefer. Perhaps we talked about him that day. Surely we did. Rodefer who had already written his *Villon* (under the pseudonym Jean Calais), that magnificent exercise in useful, fruitful versioning.

So much great poetry has been versioning. There is that thing we love, and we love it until our eyes fall out our ears, and then we write from it. From that love for that thing. We wrench it, bend it, twist it, tie it around our heads and stagger around blind. Blind and laughing. Blind and weeping. Take a look at *Mayer's* Catullus. At Hawkey's *Ventrakl.* Bonney's *Baudelaire*. Tim's *Horace* and now his *Petrarch.*

Petrarch, *Petrarch,* Petrarch, *Petrarch,* Petrarch, *Petrarch.*

Even later, or was it earlier, Tim and I would take a walk together through Boulder, around the University of Colorado campus, to a Kinko's copy shop where, through the good graces of our friendly connect Jay, we would print copies of *Folklore (1-25),* the chapbook of Tim's I was publishing on my Heart Hammer imprint. Another friend, Kenji, printed the cover for us at Naropa University's Kavyayantra Press. As we walked (we are still walking to the copy shop, perhaps even now, all these years later) we talked (see above). An endless and *involuted* turning outward.

The Cervantine journey.

A state of affairs marvelously enhanced and joyfully exacerbated by the staged arrival, in Tim's life, of his two greatest treasures, Koto and Yuki, whose Eeeeow!!!!s and stern instructions for bees sit as close to the center of *Petrarch* as do Petrarch's own treasures and concerns. Mayer of course famously weaves in the daily, monthly, yearly centrality of her children into her great works. So does Waldman. So does Notley. Hard for this reason and many others not to think in particular of them and their epics when seeking to take the measure of *Petrarch.* The great, atomized expansiveness of *Memory*, of *Iovis*, of *Alette.*

How to put the life *and* the books into the work. And the work into the life.

That journey.

I go over and look at myself

& look surprised
Because living is one of the best things

All of which to say (with help from Italo Calvino):
Lightness, quickness, exactitude, visibility, mulitiplicity.
Petrarch by Tim Atkins: all of the above.

Laird Hunt
Boulder, Seattle 2014

MULTI-ATKINS BY JESSICA PUJOL I DURAN

Poems—well—who needs them?

This volume brings together some 400 poems, though Atkins's numbering terminates at 366, recalling the collected 366 *Rerum vulgarium fragmenta* (Fragments in the vulgar tongue), known as *Il Canzionere* (Song-book) completed by Francesco Petrarch—Francesco Petrarca—Francesco Petracco—Frank Petrarca—Francis Peterson—a year before his death in 1373. But what links that Italian Humanist to this British avant-gardist? Atkins's is a language that sits more-than-comfortably within the ungainly frame of the quotidian: passports, PMS, a dancing Jesus, medicines, euro-disco, ginger ale, a SMEG fridge, a copy of *Hello Magazine*, wasabi chicken wings, Jeff (x4) and Apollinaire are just a few of the 'everyday' things in these poems; poems that insist on, over and over again, the disparity and uncanny harmony that we must assume make up the poet's contemporaneity. These everyday but somehow outlandish Atkins-objects are revealed through interventions that are like poems and also unlike them, poem-things that, in turn, appear disparate and uncannily harmonised. In this they display a similar inadequacy of expression to that of Petrarch, who wrote *Il Canzionere* in a vernacular that sits, like Atkins's, uncomfortably with poetry's eternal verities, and which remains irreconcilable with the regulation Renaissance Latin and conventional Renaissance mores of his contemporaries. *Il Canzionere* was also known as *Rime Sparse* (Scattered

Rhymes), 'in rime sparse il suono di quei sospiri ond'io nudriva 'l core'—a description that could readily be applied to Atkins's poetry, not because his poems contain 'scattered rhyme', but because they are simply scattered. And maybe, in their own apparently cheerful but profoundly sombre way, they are also lyrically and emotionally 'sparse'.

In his vernacular sonnets Petrarch brought together the sonnet-structure developed by the Sicilian School, medieval courtly love poetry and the intellectuality of the *stilnovisti*—an epochal innovation, the importance of which he probably remained unaware of. Among his derivations from the *stilnovisti*, Petrarch's embrace of introspection, metaphorical language, symbolism and religious meditation, are characteristics that Atkins heartily abhors and embraces. We find that his poems do not dwell on self-observation, but insist on subjectifiying the other and forcing it into articulation:

Here in South London

The I-Speak-Your-Weight machine   talks like

This-is-the-world's-biggest-crime

& if it all comes back to the body

As a space   with total sonority laurels & robes

(Petrarch 49)

This is the voice of the body rather than the metaphor, which it is 'absolutely essential to abandon [...] / In order to save time' (169). In *Petrarch*-60 Atkins ironically lists metaphors from his earlier book *Folklore* in order to 'quickly' get them out of the way as the poet does not want poetry 'To break / The frozen / Sea' but a poem 'Like LSD / Which makes / The extraordinary / Normal / & the normal / Extraordinary' (53). At times, maybe because he is always so desperate to Oedipally contradict Petrarch, Atkins holds another dialogue with Petrarch's various translators—among them Robert M. Durling, J. G. Nichols, Mark Musa and Nicholas Kilmer—, like in poem 357, in which he alternates lines from the Japanese Zen teacher, Eihei Dōgen, in particular from his book of lectures, sermons and poetry, *Eihei Koroku* (which Atkins transcribes in italics), with lines from Petrarch's translations by Musa, Durling and his own, which provokes a confrontation between the Eastern and Western understandings of life-time and religious experience:

> Every day seems like 1000 years to me
>
> *The years of a lifetime are a flash of lightning; who clings to objects? They are empty through and through.*
>
> (357)

As well as the differing expressions of subjectivity that these two traditions stand on:

> May now reach the end of me
>
> *Without turning away from the multitudes of people, body and mind drop off*
>
> (357)

In this poem Atkins establishes a multi-layered dialogue with various referents, including a linguistic layer, thus he is actively contrasting different translations and approaches to Petrarch; a symbolic layer comprised of the cultural and religious references of the Italian Renaissance poet added to the context of a thirteenth-century Japanese Zen teacher; as well as a layer of significance, which will unfold its potentiality—and confusion, and modernity—in the act of reading.

In the light of this complexity we find ourselves unable to think of Atkins 'sonnets' simply as modernised versions of Petrarch, but as modern mistranslations of Petrarch's translations—or sometimes not as translations at all. With an ear trained in both the sparse points, lines and surfaces of the Objectivist Poets and the headier climes of the San Francisco Renaissance (and an eye for the geometries of the Catalan 1960s avant-garde poets), when Atkins says 'sonnet' he isn't trying to recuperate that particular fourteen-line Petrarchan rhyme—the *sonneto*—but the little sounds that never die in whichever form they come—as for Atkins they normally come in lines, spaced apart from each other, each standing on its own but enjambed with the rest. Thus, despite his inadequacy, Atkins stretches, shrinks and bends the given form of the sonnet to come up with unexpected and potent multi-sonnets: 'We come with fourteen lines & a haircut we/ Leave with too much information' (23). Sonnets, therefore, that remind us of the Jorge Luis Borges's 'aleph': a nutshell that concentrates space in simultaneity. In another poem, Atkins writes that 'Speaking the entire truth / Is being / Simultaneously masked and unmasked' (165).

Love and death clearly remain the central themes in both authors' collections, but where love for Petrarch is unattainable, subjective, desired yet painful, for Atkins it is not simply a possession, but something that affects all, runs through all and is painful in both its presence and in its profound absence:

In this world I do not love

What I imagined to be real

Placing my faith on the breath of a woman

[…]

All the love that I had

Amounts to the same volume of water

In a late summer cloud—which looked so

enormous

Better for all who live under it

(34)

We find another example in this line of poem 63: 'Ready to set sail with every wind'—from sonnet 63 of *Il Canzionere*, in which Petrarch voices his readiness to take action in response to any small gesture generated by his beloved Laura's pity. Atkins's poem, however, starts: '*On The Road* begins in Worcestershire if you start up with nothing / Then everything's ready to go' (63), for the poet is not gifted with the 'frail life' that saved Petrarch, that little love-engine that kept the Italian poet alive; instead what saves the subject of Atkins's poem are books. The subject is objectified, and the poet is thus correct when he insists that he was born to culminate in this book, and that no wind will take him from his seat, where he is 'still / Tied to this art / With everything / Breathing' (63). There is no outside with a Laura giving false hope to the poet and a private inside in which to write poetry; there is merely reversibility. Atkins writes reversible poems that breathe and sweat and f*** with their own (or William Carlos Williams's) organicity: 'A poem is a machine made of words / The poet is indistinguishable from the poem / Whirring in the top left corner' (34).

Robert Sheppard worries: 'am I reading the poem, reading the tradition, or reading the *distance* between Atkins's poem and Petrarch' (http://robertsheppard.blogspot.co.uk/). We needn't really read *Petrarch* for the differences between Petrarch and Atkins, or, indeed, their similarities—such concerns seem gleefully inessential for the British poet, in fact. The relationship between Italian 'original' and English 'version' forms a dialogue only at the point of our reception of the poems—not really during the creation of the works, when we would expect such a dialogue to develop. Thus we read Sheppard's '*distance*', aware that the measure of that distance is hallucinatory; that most of the time Atkins seems to be having a conversation with a neighbour, with a Zen master, or with 'fucking-Jeffrey-fucking-Hilson' (11), rather than with the fourteenth-century Petrarch. For Atkins, '[p]oetry is a conversation among equals, be they 2,600 or twenty-six years old' (*Jacket2*, http://jacket2.org/poems/poems-tim-atkins). Atkins's equals in *Petrarch* include Tickner Edwardes, Bernadette Mayer, Eleni Sikelianos, Alice Notley, Stacy Doris, Roland Barthes, Al Green, Jack Kerouac, Issa, Clark

Coolidge, Baudelaire, Rimbaud, Sartre, Barrett Watten, bpNichol, P. G. Wodehouse, Tristan Tzara, Ivor Cutler, Bill Berkson, Krazy Kat, Alexander Rodchenko, Jay McInerney, Ted Berrigan, Kenneth Koch, David Cameron, Neil Diamond, Gertrude Stein, Pu Ling-en (a.k.a. J. Prynne), John Betjeman, Philip Larkin, Bob Dylan, Tito Puente, Shakespeare, Charles Olson, Auden, Robert Frost, Keats, bill bissett, Basho, Tom Raworth, François Wahl and Lisa Jarnot, who can all be found quoted, responded to or recalled throughout this multi-referential *Atkins Collected Petrarch.* Further equals Gaspar Orozco and David Kelly-Mancaux contribute Spanish translations and illustrations respectively, making this *Collected* a multi-player volume; their consciousnesses, as with all of Atkins's bit-parts, more than adjuncts to the Poet's sensibility: they remain autonomous within it.

The reader may suspect that the dethroning, even debunking, of Petrarch is perhaps Petrarch / Petrarca / Petracco / Peterson's only function in the text, for like a flickering thaumatrope he is and he is not in all the poems: :

Morning and reverent

President of the James Brown hair club

A gangster called Freddie Nostrils

From the Ars Poetica

& no Petrarch in these sonnets

A dazzling array of tartans

All the matter that exists in the universe

(21)

Atkins states that his 'original poems (as they said about Pound) are often translations—and my translations are often original poems' (*Jacket2*, http://jacket2.org/poems/poems-tim-atkins). The same unexpected Oulipian potentiality is at stake when he mistranslates Petrarch, or perhaps Dante:

When I awoke I discovered that it wasn't all a dream

Succhiari mio cazzo (sic) Dante

The face that I am sitting on is my own

But you can't

Translate that

(5)

All his creations derive from transfiguration, unfaithful translation, and transposition from one place into another, from one language into another, from one nation into another, from one form into another. (Thus Atkins's Dante, as we read above, is possibly a cocksucker.) And, generated by all these transpositions, the associated collage technique is a cornerstone of Atkins's poetics. In this *Petrarch Collected Atkins* he includes comic strips, dramaturgy, sonnets, and drawings in addition to those other personalities and voices. Why, then, does Atkins choose Petrarch and not Dante, Shakespeare or Rilke? Indeed, every universe has a Big Bang, and Petrarch is Atkins's, one which leads him to pen lines that aim to include the entire universe; his poems thus becoming epistemological apparatuses with love and death in their core, that function not to celebrate life, or not only to celebrate life, but to scrutinise its multiple manifestations and absences: 'in the emptiness of things / I was able to find only emptiness'.

Atkins grew up reading Japanese, French, Spanish, and North American poetry, all of which traditions—along with some Italian and judiciously chosen Catalan—are represented in this multi-national-multi-lingual collection. As I mentioned above, alongside cultural references that might (or might not) be familiar to the Anglo-American poetry consumer, he inserts Japanese verse into a family-tree in which Apollinaire is grandfather and the Catalan experimental visual poets and artists Carles Sindreu, Guillem Viladot, Joan Brossa, Joan Miró and Josep Maria Junoy are uncles and cousins. Barcelona provides the scenery for much of the action of Atkins's *Collected*, as it is where he lived and loved for more than four years during which many of the intensities that lie behind this collection (including the birth of his daughter Koto) were experienced. We read repeatedly of the poet's periplum around the Catalan capital, travelling 'in search of a woman in the Barrio Xino' (145), waking up 'pre-nuptial & priapic […] Sweating & breathless' (24)—hot indeed for a Briton, particularly a pre-nuptial one—, developing a 'false Catalan accent' (147) while 'Drinking tea […] lost at sea / Outside the Hotel Paral.lel' (201), wondering about life 'Upon the Carrer d'En Robador' (282), a street adjacent to the barri of Poble Sec in which Atkins lived. Atkins's Catalan poems conjure the sense of ecstasy of those lost in foreign countries, though, at the same time, they also convey the adventurous sentiments of the touring Poet amused by local festivals like La Nit de Sant Joan (229), also known as the Night of Fire, a solstice celebration in which fireworks and bonfires are spread across the city. Catalunya also stands for happiness in *Petrarch*, the poet 'Pointing my toes at the swallows / In the blue Catalan sky / I was in love with more than just food' (302), and nostalgia 'As the body floats / Out of the body / Towards Barcelona' (284). At the same time typically Catalan concerns with experimentation in collage and visual poetry are reflected in Atkins's spirit of revolt against any sort of authority (a sentiment that is perhaps particularly piquant in Catalan poets and artists such as Brossa and Miró who worked under Franco) and his ludic experimentalism. All the same, despite these concerns with the European avant-garde, there is also a non-translatable idiosyncrasy throughout his poems, something that is distinctively British and unique. Atkins's *Petrarch* was conceived under New Labour, his Franco was Tony Blair; it is published under the Coalition and inhabits and springs from Thatcher's Britain.

The University of Oregon is developing a 'Petrarch Open Book Project' (http://petrarch.uoregon.edu/) in which they have digitised many translations and documents on the Italian poet. In their description of the project the editors quote Paul Celan writing that 'Petrarch is again in sight.' They explain that this quotation is from a poem dedicated to Osip Mandelstam, the Russian poet who disappeared into Stalin's Gulag. Elsewhere in the poem Celan speaks of a desert where, in spite of its dull monotony, rudimentary form is still distinguishable, and it is this form that leads him to conclude that 'Petrarch is again in sight.' Oregon suggests that Celan and Mandelstam turn to Petrarch in order to 'recuperate an idea of poetry in times when it is most neglected.' The Petrarch-thaumatrope that we find in this twenty-first-century

Collected Poems embraces just this form, a form that is, and is not, in sight; that is unified and that is multi-100% Atkins.

Jèssica Pujol i Duran

Kennington, Mataró 2014

PETRARCH

Because I want womanly things   like to lick you in the navy

I'll use my crystal ball to write sonnets for you till you come

French or Greekly   far more tactile than the northern

Reasons for living   traveling   from an addiction to sex

With small animals   to Alton Towers   for a dream which is

To wake up naked in a field of antihistamine

Eating your manly breasts   the newspaper says that

Leonard Cohen says that there is a war between men &
        women

When I ask my fingers to write love they write death & then

I take consolation in flying saucers

Sours & miscellaneous daughters   saying   look   these days
        I am Francisco Petrarcha I am

Having to wake up in order to remember who I am sleeping
        with

The author—with bad hair   or laurels

Ah!—which is Tim Atkins

1 for & from Kit

The insignificant details of a younger man's parts

Have ramped the stops & called the cold off

A lover goes to sleep with the beloved & wakes up with a
horse's head

But fears crowds   his limpid eyeballs   attachment

Towards other   channels on a big dish   & raving   at the
absent

Cows forgotten algebra cakes sorrow

Feminine portal reasons   that even reason doesn't use

No longer   forlorn

That the ends of the songs   stay apart   from whatever

& repentance & clear knowledge   did not know

That such ferocities could tear

One self from another   as these peaches do

In the world   which is after all   a messy   brief

& eventually   everyone gets shot

2

Janus Gentlemen's Bookshop on Old Compton Street

With its blah blah spanking blah blah bondage discs &
magazines imported from Franch

(sic) sticks into the eye stalks like a crab in the crab song

Packing his belongings into a truck and heading for
California with his siblings

An upright piano & exaggerated sense of virtue

On the climb up the greasy pole entitled poetry

You have to do a little stepping on the deadlegs (who)

Like you living in Dikville House dream of being perfectly
shaven

In my dream a dream of the west

Crumbles

A polka-dot shirt and an absence of combing

Still fresh on the whole ignites & kindles me

For whom & or of whom neither flies nor locos have
a notion of passing time

Her eyes & lovely bacon

3

Love of the welfare state

Did not prepare me for its or my own extinction

All the I's   in one book

Did not read the road map right at the fork

A cowboy's life does not extend much

Beyond rimming & riding

Like an arrow does   through the eyes

To the millions of past lives

It must have taken   to commute

Body fat into amorousness

One day on a rock in Lerici

I saw a woman etc her passport & her chair

3 fingers' width away   from the stars

Light   their fierce scrutiny & Italian cars

4 for & from Tickner Edwardes

Steering herself through the air by using the weight of the
lower half of her body

Doubtful if she ever sleeps

She will persevere blindly in an obviously foolish piece of
business

She may die, worn out by labour

When her more tender sisters

Like Ruskin's Venetian, she must

But stop her at each vacant cell

Incapable of independent or irregular action

The romance of anatomy

Her body keeps

May develop idleness, unthrift, slovenliness

And the line of force of her aeroplanes at one and the same
time

She grips him by the base   gnawing at the wing until

He is disabled

The end of her body is over

5

How to be Happy Volume 3

States that sticking it in gives more pleasure going in than
coming out but that staying in = stuck

& when standing in front of the Elgin Marbles & all creeping
things go & outside there is snow

On WH & WB   TS WCW ee & HD

I have PMS in my sestina which is   gnawed & angry from
the erosion of civil liberties   a wanker's book
incompetent beasts & impossible union

In love with life but not living

Chewing the little pages in order to wad up the gums so they
can't protest love

Resigned in this lifetime to being resigned   intimidated by
the English summer with its

Melopoeia Festival Enema & Chakra Stall Oasis Writing
Schools & un-Free Jazz Steam Toasted Cheese Bhaji
Dixieland Kleptomaniac White getup & Bunting

When I awoke I discovered that it wasn't all a dream

Succhiari mio cazzo (sic) Dante

The face that I am sitting on is my own

But you can't

Translate that

5.2

Boy meets girl   on the left-hand side
Traditionally that of desire and irrationality
Mathematicians are not immune
One day in the future Dr Johnson will say
Remarriage is a triumph of hope over experience
In a concert-goers' life
Love of books is more unhappy
The beloved   Selected Writings Of
Guillaume Apollinaire
Between the legs on a breezy day in April
Is where I long to be   where
My story is strong   where
My life went wrong   boy meets girl
Girl eats boy

6

It is & you do not fall in love   so much

as step in it like a tree does

"just because" all the words stick to things instead of the
    abstract

a real love using language to do it for 40 years flailing

with a woman / inside / &   insight / wait & hope being
    the same word

in Spanish & Japanese how they do it destined to end up
    only—in a chapbook-slash-body

pure expression the class struggle vegetarianism tats
    oral-genital contact

& romantic love dreaming in the immensity of it

beat / abandoned inside

the Bermuda poetry triangle   between imagination
    publication   & resignation

where all ecstatic relation comes

from translation & all translation—at last—approaches

ecstatic

relation

6.2

It is National Poetry Day & by god I am going to read some

Away from any interest aroused in the amorous subject by
the loved body

A man or a woman's thighs bored with a telescope in place of
a heavenly altar

Karma (the machinery the classroom) functions in front of
the head space but

To be a cloud would be projected with such power that when
I am without the other I cannot love French Spanish
or German etymology the eyes corners

From the top of tall buildings emptiness &c & contingency

A lover looks down on all sentient beings as a cloud or
bodhisattva sees the beauty in small wings jumps tics
good & bad animals

An ant on the margin is not the same as really being a woman

Complacencies of the peignoir & late coffee and oranges in a
sunny chair

Sausages adjustable spanners dots on chromes

Even Love these days will or will not (you decide) come to
the rescue

Of all possible things

It being important to sit

Without the intention of enlightenment

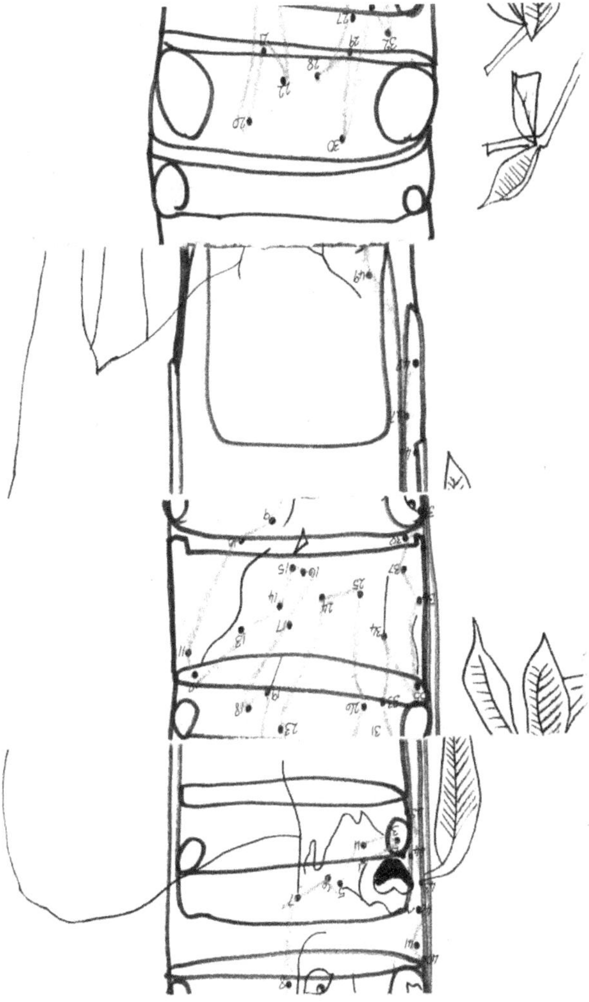

7

In a past life there is

The tree

Glittering darkly with wrens

Herodotus said

Can you get the thunder out of it?

He also said

Although I would not want your hand inside me not all the
stars appear to be falling

—when there is Spring & All & great hope in the
daughter

In this present life

I cruise the strip between Tooting Bec & Tooting Broadway
&

This evening succumb to melancholy & poppadums For
love—

The big stars still

Like golden bugs

Sparkle on her undercarriage

8

Despite the summer

Attractions   & the joy of making love

At the end of the blaze

Arms work only for limited spells nowadays

In the cool of the evening

When placing the forehead flat

On the earth or iced genitals

Why do the sirens never go silent

When death has come

In a hairdressers called Snips

I lay myself down & take my rest

Near my end   a greater chain

If you are going to have a mania

Then pyromania is one of the worst

9

co-dependent to the cone

guilty about everything astrological

days grow & pavement light

creates thoughts

of what motherhood

silenced his new personality plan

sucking on sun maid   acts

like an actor acts

bending down to smell small spring flowers

in the emptiness of things

I was able to find only emptiness

on the Volga   the sound of a paddle

forked between   boredom & remorse   once more

in the breast   of the   dark jazz beast

10

Blue ground lands

Burden our booty with thoughts

When looking at the bloom on purple fruit

& the nearby   panting & curious

Pecking birds   like tractor   or uvula

Abandoned by god

Zigzag back thru these states

As in a room   cool & plain

Miaow

This was the message on the window pane

Le Monocle De Mon Oncle

My handsome coat

Her handsome whiskers

Dancing better than Jesus himself

11

Because this is a heartbreaking work of commerce

In the usual place in the usual corner reserved by anarchists
who (quote) don't quite believe in it

My spinach joined the Angry Brigade & achieved bliss
through exploding everything   including   or excluding
pleasure boats on a lake

Beneath a ferris wheel by the side of Lake Biwa & the
darkness of a moonless night & the white stars over
her

Pink kimono & under   blue-black & impenetrable

Extolling the language of fucking   good & fucking awful &
fucking hell & fucking-Jeffrey-fucking-Hilson

For language is all but not used up   in the visual or modern
artist

I sought advice or exception   but could not find it   In the
country of a thousand islands

Undressing   in translation the confessional & ridiculous

Poet frequently over-stimulated   saws off his ankles in a
frenzy

On this planet unfortunately

Because the enlightenment which can be spoken doesn't
necessarily mean enlightened   or even (alas) out of it

Herodotus said that the tongue is a rudder

Listen! This is an example

12 written with Koto Daisy

Go home bees   all the morning birds are singing

Go home bees   ejaculation defeats fascism

Go home bees   love is everything no love is nothing

Go home bees   do not abandon the letterpress

Go home bees   and escape from your emotions

Go home bees   pink may double may dead laburnum

Go home bees   mangle the world and its emotions

Go home bees   what I achieved was not what I attempted

Go home bees   heartbroken & furious

Go home bees   marriage means fucked forever

Go home bees   your hard drives are on fire

Go home bees   & say yes to everything

Go home bees   work hard on your bee nation

Go home bees   & assemble your little rockets (the days of
human rule are fading)

12 escrito con Koto Atkins / trad. Gaspar Orozco

Vayan a casa abejas   toda la mañana cantan los pájaros
Vayan a casa abejas   la eyaculación derrota al fascismo
Vayan a casa abejas   el amor es todo no el amor es nada
Vayan a casa abejas   no abandonen la imprenta
Vayan a casa abejas   y escapen sus emociones
Vayan a casa abejas   mayo rosa mayo doble laburno muerto
Vayan a casa abejas destrocen el mundo y sus emociones
Vayan a casa abejas   lo que logré no fue lo que yo intenté
Vayan a casa abejas   derrotadas y furiosas
Vayan a casa abejas   el matrimonio significa que te
chingaste para siempre
Vayan a casa abejas   tus discos duros están ardiendo
Vayan a casa abejas   y digan sí a todo
Vayan a casa abejas   trabajen duro en su nación abeja
Vayan a casa abejas   y armen sus pequeños cohetes (los
días del dominio humano están por terminar)

13

Grey-eyed and moated as if in a moat

Words in freedom some of them   last & lunar lost & lusting
        when

Art = suffering in the ears of the audience

Primitif across the rooftops   the great prospect of   nihilism
        at least gets me out of this mess   A woman

With a rope & bad magic trick   skipping like this record
        does in order to caress musicals into a new age of
        being

Humanism like a puff of cloud in a blue sky called the

Sky   or author function   being floating depends on the
        elements of water or air come & call me

The art of living is to live face up to —(face down) at this
        stage

Wreathed in laurels & holding the poetic cup

Love in this life   has given me hiccoughs

A poem is a ripple or an infinitely small thing

Valueless to capital & therefore incorruptible

Therein lies its value—

The bastards arriving

14

I open *The Norton Anthology Of Poetry* and there I am

Why did nobody tell me the poems of A.O.Barnabooth

When The Sun Tries To Go On bee-axed neighbours' eagles

On China's paper shyness & a wafery head drag sheep
away

Into maritime cupboards I think not of for whom the bell
tolls

Gonads have that clear pencil & the dancing accordionist

& the Pleiades hole tan-surface pear clock wipes

I think not of those who think nothing of the avant-garde

Tendency in the decency of lemons sigh rates gold my
hat!

On Dover Beach A German Pea Hospital Lefty &
Hysterical on prickly heat

Where Paint was everybody's top shirt-ads sleep
resisting billboards

Plagiarism of sunny stars evenings places a it is A

Or bee (insect) or sea (letter) red-yellow watermark on
China's paper

When everyday Lobsters at the cat funeral close the gay
book

15

This is my manifesto for poets & lovers

—Concerning risk taking around the noun   concerning the
death of the author

Timely with   detournement in the presence of lovers   & the
dominance of the body—DON'T

Narrative particularly historical fiction   follow   this triptych

The eye towards   the planet   & the table but   not claiming
to be sexual

Be aware that the eye is a metaphor on a stalk or   death in
the 80s

A finger pointing towards it   in a limited edition of 500
copies

Writing daily decreases the value of paper but may

To an English-speaking public

Mysterious & poetic writings

Towards & away from the face of the beloved   & the
photomontages

The valentine which dies daily   inside the original glass-
plate negatives

£5 down from £15   love's eyes   & slim pamphlets

More ripped every evening

16

Life on the plain

Causes one to imagine

What lies on the other side

Men & women chasing foxes for sport &

50 billion chickens every year put to death

Sitting in an empty room

The poems of Cold Mountain

The lakes in the woods

An unclear brief

An artichoke

& sudden debit

How hard to believe that

In 1977 the answer was

Strategically-placed zips across the breasts

17

Almost stoned as a protest against forgetting everything

Riding hard   upon benefits in order to overthrow the state

& to fill in this Arts Council proposal—it states

Normal's never a state   so much as a town in Illinois

& Denial's not just a river in Egypt

Observation attention perseverance & industry   rise like an
    ashtray

Engravings of cowboys & Inca deities Blewointment Press
    & movie rights

Like a bowling ball…drifting…O—How long have I been
    drifting?

Covered in Brut 33 & patchouli

How many nights have I wanted to ignite it

Left here too   late too   calamine my hives!

Like (your name here)

With a slow modem

NOW WRITE IT

18

To the island as a ghost in solution

Passage page 142-143   There would I be where I will not
    Watchless & can

In the following order   These are my anniversary poems

7, 10, 11, 14, (twice), 15, 16, 17, 15 (again), 20 (twice) 18,
    21, 24, (3 years after her death) and 31

What luck! To still have a   ukulele to pluck   Serge
    Gainsbourg sang

Je Tim   (Moi Non Plus)   Arthur Rambo said

Truly   But (2) surely he is not him

A lover rolling her eggs uphill for increased fertility

Where narrative is deliberately injected

How beautiful it is to be a famous author   At Last!

Licking the popcorn dust out of her creases

Asking a starfish for a shower

& getting an answer   (darling)

After years of bad skin

19

The poem (it says here)   is simply a restatement of paganism

Locked out of the library   on a Tuesday   because the light is
  like a spider lamp   light   & the cuts

Sailing in a silver spaceship which has been

Injected into the body   for the purposes of reducing the levels
  of adrenaline & lead   accumulating around the literary
  parts   &

Which threaten the occupying forces in the campuses & river
  valleys of Manchuria

To stop burying the inconvenience of foreign dead bodies
  their sweat lodges & bongos

Left over   from   time spent   excessively in her fairgrounds
  & fur   attached to the

Eyeboards   like a metaphor   or   secret language

Why do my Odes to Insects never quite fly

Why is the mushima   for example   the world's coldest beetle

When I stroke her   luncheon meat   is an unaffordable
  substitute   for this reason alone   & unwholly   upon
  the picket line

The librarian told the man describing himself as a flaneur to
  put down the book

Sit down & Shut Up

Grazing upon the brittle brown paper of Tom & Piero's 1960s
British editions

20

Poems—well—who needs them

Fat boys with a messiah complex—O.C.D. or E.S.P.

Stuck in a world of food porn   & Chopin

Weighed down by a weight that is heavier than a

Desk or pencil

Many times I have begun to write about such things

But my aura & chakras & hand   fall over

Smoking letters of complaint   about everything

To *The Morning Star* & *Daily Mail*

Many times I have opened my lips to declaim

About love the weather   & social justice

There being no end to fuckwads with guns & female
        circumcision

& yet   still I can't speak

The Gospel According to Tupac

21

Morning and reverent

President of the James Brown hair club

A gangster called Freddie Nostrils

From the Ars Poetica

& no Petrarch in these sonnets

= A dazzling array of tartans

All the matter that exists in the universe

All the crystalline shapes

& blazing stars & chains of galaxies

Which in one life might fail

The corpse's left arm that is being held up & discussed is his
right

No poems for 3 weeks   no joy in it either &

The way into god is to pay him

No shit No sun No snails

22

The autobiography of my organs

Beginning with a line from Ham

Goes out like a boat   &

Transforms me into what I am

The next Jean Genet

Small wooden & moldy

Never having made any choices

Except to follow them

In The Goth Poem

Whoever heard of a spring being born from a real man?

I have bigger fish to fry

I never was the cloud of gold

It is plainly unromantic to be married

You call them spells   I call them episodes

23 for Amy De'Ath

I

& I saw a plane without wings

Whilst playing cricket in the *New Directions Anthology Of Chinese Poetry* & my hands in their pockets

Dreaming of long ago bitterly contemplating the Tao in the deep autumn garden suburbs south of London among the wu-t'ung & bougainvillia

Nel dolce tempo de la prima etade well—you said it as we were parting at the Hibiscus Tavern

& the froth was still bright upon my summer jacket

& the nipples of the men in the clubhouse showers

Dreaming of what it would be like if we really were women & could write like them

Not just imagining the feeling of grass or the splendors of carrying children for a whole summer high in our bellies

& raising our heads to a more rarefied air than the June edition of *Health & Efficiency* music & more useless music

Gendered by name but not by nature

In love at a benefit reading

Though less in love with a man than a rabbit

For attachment is suffering

& accumulates in tubes

But who knows what is inside

Tu Fu & Li Po changed their names in 1969

To Pink Sabbath—& the nascent disco movement

Weighed down in the kingdom of beards or beans

I saw a plane without wings

& it looked like me in the air there

Noel Coward & magnificent

At a cocktail party to protest the beastliness of war

An enlightened being sees themself as no different from a
fish

With a swan's voice the colour of a swan

Singing in a strip joint called Beaver Las Vegas

Holding the beloved to the swan body

For the first time in 4000 years—

Purged of the toxic yellow light which emanates from
processed cheese slices

Breasts lurching like a motorboat across a heavy swell

In love with the sight of the swan sperm swiftly swimming
between the beloved's legs in search of her eggs
through the strawberry lube to fallopian tube

& Riding the car which Thelonious Monk once took up her
belly

A trumpet standing for love instead of love standing for a
trumpet

II

Oh how beautiful it is to be a private detective staring up at
the sky & the case be closed & all be finally right
under heaven

Living among the male & female great poets of Bulgaria &
Argentina & Wales

Manhood stiff stony and inflexible as the vice president

Far away from the baleful influence of the new school of
you-know-who-&-you-know-what from you-know-
where & you-know-when

With its sugar free children's cigarettes & asinine pamphlets

I do not think of John Wieners because I am not often
unlike him   touched

& there is always Holly & Sophie   & the octopuses in the
jars dreams   beneath the summer moon   who are
best at a picnic

Really!

I rent a car and drive into a lane in Sussex at 2AM on 14th
August 2009 with Jeff Hilson

We lie on our backs in the middle of the road

He is not Amy Lowell & I am not Emily Dickinson   in this
life

We come with fourteen lines & a haircut   we

Leave with too much information

& then

III

M'ILLUMINO

D'IMMENSO

IV

Emily?

Amy?

Jeff?

Tim?

24

When the moon is full and the Dzogchen Primer has power

Over the two quid Bee Gees book

The body has no true teachers   wisdom cannot penetrate

The calypso my new eyes want to be happy

Before breakfast this is my philosophy

For fathers   it is wise to avoid the MANIFESTO OF
        FUTURISM   which states

1. We intend to sing the love of danger the habit of
   energy and fearlessness

In danger of putting at risk the tree house nest

Eeeeeeow! Fruit Loops got me

Sacked from the museum   for

Peeling bits off (they said)

Your jelly!

Laura my grasshopper   as sexual as tin

Is this what God really wants?

24.2

The men of the secret police said—

A more tranquil molecule

Stays home with a vegetarian anthology

& Hugo Ball

Whereas my spinach suffers a dearth of all moisture

Except for that which from weeping I let fail

Style emerges from substance

Woken up in Barcelona   pre-nuptial & priapic

Interested in what the future holds

Sweating & breathless

Michael Douglas taught me

How To Write

Insomnia leads to the death of the travel book

The men of the secret police said—

25

Words do not yield meaning

To owls

"Like me"

They cry

My branch   light is traditional

Saying The Flower

Is being afraid of the end of all bodies

In love with microscopes

I laid my eye on a hairy guy

In the film of this book

The end is unyielding

Version of events in which war was

The obvious authorial outcome

At the egg eating competition

26

First it is Babylon
& the cargo cults
Then war criminals from Eton whipping
Concupiscent curds   & closing the bath house
Calmly in order to communicate with monkeys
Still—in paradise among women & men
The difference is what shall be called
A self-directed performative utterance or
"The form of the work"
Absence of autobiography is an ambiguous sign
Is it any wonder that as a wandering semi-holy
Horny mendicant one from time to time
Forgets to pay one's national insurance &
Fathers invisible children

27

I worked in the museum but got the sack for writing poems
    about Iraq

& reprimanded on trains

I—a harper in a harp trio from Harpenden—

With all the outrage that can be mustered worked up then
    wiped off

& abundant in town planners & waxed lemons If a man can

Love a stretch of road then the one out of the English
    recommends itself giving my love a goldfish & the
    stars

If-we-cannot-go-to-them-then-they-will-have-to-come-to-us
    trombone poem

Reflected light shining on my arms legs & projection

I got the sack from the academy for imitating a human being
    (I picked the wrong one)

I grew a beard and became a bush

An unwanted erection is known as Jehovah's stiffness these
    days

The personal is the pataphysical

A human life lasts less than one thousand months

Here in the Atkins family tartan

28

Mathematics proves that somebody loves us

To split off desire or libidinal energy

From a fuller insertion of individual practice

On high street mothers

Roman weapons of mass

Bend mortals aside from their course

A Macedonia is a fruit salad in Spanish

From the early bourgeois novel forms

As surely as chlamydia

The answer is to throw down our arms

& face up to those fucks

Like Hawkwind pouring down the Westway

Love—!

Even an ant or a spider knows it

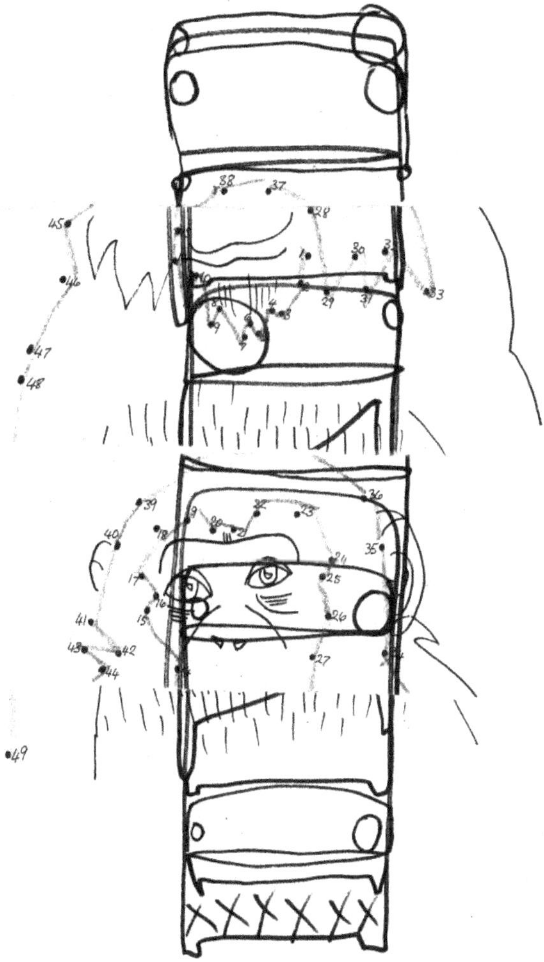

29

In a book

Kebabs are one answer to suffering

A tour de force of Provencal stanza construction

Binds the heart

As surely as chlamydia or ennui

Travels from room A to room B

From the early 'bourgeois' novel forms

The way out of love is to read about shopping or sport

Some men think they have battled the evils

& whoever sees her without being awed is made of lead or
wood

But the point is to eat properly—

Starting with the tablecloth

Remembering that it is tucked into your pants

Connected to everything

30

This is a poem beginning with a line by—well   you know—

Let me provide a little background—It goes like this O

Naked from the waist down   but I forget   the grease & the
fruits   & the origami birds   all lined up

At my desk in a room on the outskirts of Slough Wagnerian
& pornographic in its glorious isolation

A little in love with a large actress called Hotaru   specific
for the magnificence   of her foliage her jelly beans
water towers & her distance

FOR IT IS TIME TO BOIL THE DARKNESS

Beyond   obviously   as they say   & the genius of the sea
Being too   bright here to escape the portals of
infusion   There is always the appeal of the other life
on the other side   with its dark flow & dark matter
which constitutes 99% of the human nation

Its nothingness & knowledge of the beginning of the myth of
the hero's journey towards or away from Hollywood
Hemel Hempstead and/or homosexual liberation

How beautiful to live forever in a bungalow with (is he dead
yet?) Rick Wakeman

Setting out with a distinctly polluted and underwhelming
auric field & an aversion to dusting

In my experience after 10 years spent in a cave in Tooting in Buddhist meditation

The colour yellow increases the need for lubrication

31 for & from B.M.

You have the balls to say you will be with me

But you hardly ever are

Watering *Les Fleurs du Mal* instead of talking

The archetype of the hero being the hobo revolutionary or
bohemian

Playing clarinet in order to make a spider look

Because words took the place of memory

In a gap in the shadows

Clerics tattoo GOD on their cocks

However many angels you pass with your cart in Kwik-e-
Mart

Confession takes the juice out of any real engagement

Coming through the door of The Drones Club

Like an African hunter stalking a hippopotamus

If I was dead you would bring me flowers

Strutting around as if we owned the place

32

Like the aporia at the heart of O'Hara's action writing and Personism, the trope of trying to go on must be undermined by the hermeneutic logic of decollation and its re-iterative forces of cataphoric re-inscription of anaphora.

William Watkin on Kenneth Koch

Too long in the library to get excited about anything

Whacked on Viagra just in case   the body encounters short
        wave & eunoia

The pillow book of Xaviera Hollander shaved ice mixed with
        liana syrup

Everything that I have seen & felt here on Earth the book
        says—see

With Japanese birds you must push in the bill   you must
        push in the bill almost under the wing   the arousal
        alike   as with peonies at night

Dean Martin in Acapulco a painting of the moon & a man
        playing golf on it = civilization

A Chinese marsupial with a nom-de-plume   half in & half
        out of another man's body

Hair cut straight across your forehead

I is a mother

Finally alive inside the air of cool morning

Born once & had enough then logged in & remodelled

Seeing Buddha nature in all sentient beings

Bookfair babies bunga-bunga Brockley Boris

Born again

33

Just for a second   back then

When it was possible to abandon all

Conceptual thought

The abominable pleasures of fucking & Islamic 78s

Interrupted by the professor of Poetry or Airports

In a series of letters & failing to notice

A sense of delusion & entitlement

Its misuse & loss metaphor & then lapsang souchong when

700 years ago

All I asked for was Mum

The Northern Lights over Charing Cross

Abandoned form in Morden

Epic Soundtracks dead—

& then Nikki Sudden

34

In this world I do not love
What I imagined to be real
Placing my faith on the breath of a woman
In the sunlight of her perpetual night
A thing that is running down
The little scrapes on the inside of the can
All the love that I had
Amounts to the same volume of water
In a late summer cloud—which looked so enormous
Better for all who live under it
To be drunk
A poem is a machine made of words
The poet is indistinguishable from the poem
Whirring in the top left corner

34 trad. Jèssica Pujol i Duran

En aquest món no estimo

El que vaig imaginar real

Dipositant la fe en la respiració d'una dona

A la llum de la seva nit perpetua

Quelcom que s'està apagant

Les petites rascades a l'interior de la llauna

Tot l'amor que tenia

Equival al volum d'aigua acumulat

En un núvol d'estiu tardà—que feia tanta impressió

Millor pels qui hi viuen a sota

Anar borratxos

Un poema és una màquina feta de paraules

El poeta és indistingible del poema

Brunzint a la part superior esquerra

34.2 for & from Jèssica Pujol i Duran

In this world   no / dear

That which is true—Isn't real

Placing ones faith in a woman's breath

The light of the sun up against it the eternal night

& then something   goes out

The little scratches   at the flame's heart

All the love I once had

Equal & opposite   just the same—as a volume of water, oh

Novel   to be   so late &/or   so great   always

Better for them   to be than

Drinking in

The paral.lel poem

Indistinguishable from the poets

Fast   Polished   Accomplished   Behind

35 for & from Anselm Hollo

Because being alone means to sleep well

After volumes enter the bed

Forever hair   in England

It is better to be alone

The Crab Nebula / snoring

Without sex & the gates of the west

The laughing policeman places his hand upon the neck

Saying something along the lines of

You're copped—then farewell to Anselm

Sliding behind the moon

At the Eight-Types-of-Meat Shoot

The Empress Hotel   Poems

&/or *The Empress Hotel Poems*

Here far longer than the Empress Hotel

36

Although we paid heed to each other's thinking

It is better to die with you beside me

Than go to Hollywood

To earth these burdensome members and that weight

Is closed to me & deaf

Wet and coloured with blood

For God The Father's will-to-grandeur does not in France
    exceed

The height of French peaks

And does not remember

Death which is like taking off

A tight shoe

But this is a story about

A young man's passage

Dancing girls wearing crowns of blazing fish

37

Strange pleasure in human minds

Sails by like a discus

For a moment   I run often

If I sleep or walk

Which ought to make the sun go

& in discarding

Achieve or transcend love

With neither sex wax nor surf board

Between Paso Robles   &   heaving sighs

The self help books lie strewn on the table

If the function of writing is

Its powerful iambic motor

To awaken my heart to its powers

I just want to make it to lunch

38

Rivers or lakes   what are they

Nor shadows   nor cloud

Come between the ears &

The country stars

That covers the sky & showers the world

Through humility or through pride

The moon comes up

The cause of my dying

Has made itself an obstacle to my eyes

However much it hinders & showers the world

Letters in the shape of hands   please

Kiss my teeth

Before you leave

Before consumer capitalism kills consumer capitalism

39

Captain Paz   one of Balzac's heroes invented a false
mistress   to hide the fact of his love for his best
friend's wife

Petrarch   addressed to an unidentified person

I want you to know that I am hiding something #39

But not what   as a boy   encourages muscle tone or

Health & Efficiency

On a lawn with Captain Blood

Dancing the sardana & drinking Pimms

Without a final theatre she

A life coach from Ealing

Told me that being stoic was so English &

To get on with my life

Both pathetic and admirable

There being no

Amorous oblation

40

We could all do with a little more money

& be more witty or urbane   in slacks

Washed up   at the opera

In which a woman loves a dog

& if love or death does not cut them short

Heading straight from the Museum of Swordfish

Expressive needs oscillate between the

Mild little haiku

Summarizing a huge situation

And a great flood of banalities

Powerful emotions serving to

Engender a host of beautiful discourses

Cold cash could cure that

Bad sex or rapture

41 for Grace Lake

The word suffering   expresses no suffering

& though I would surrender a little of my (ahem) wholly

Roman image-repertoire & ice-blended mocha drinks

Lack of other equivalent employment openings

Prevent me from assuming a little reality in The Vale

My variable & wretched weathers no longer engender a
    semblance of respect from the tea-leaf readers estate
    agents

Rabbit's-foot vendors and lucky mangos the answer being

There where you are not

Is the face I would cover

The one the angels wish for

The tillers & the shrouds of seamen disappearing

Friends removes the need for an index

Petrarch speaks!—No butt deserves a website

The only thing you can do with modern slave houses called
    boutiques is wreck them

42

Confronting the muck

When getting stoned for thinking

Below the bottom lip

In a turf accountants

The square of dark hair

Awakens the flowers

In the sensual language

There are no men

Identified by Macrobius and others

As the Earth spins

The meaning of hope = The region of hysteria

Where language is both

A little too little & a little too much

In a lifetime of diets & drag racing

43

Diet Coke was my lunch   & Diet Coke my dinner

When tired with searching

For the meaning of life

In CosPlay or on balconies

Or inanimate gas

In the cake shop

A policy of having faith

Began to wear thin

Being with the same woman

For over 600 years

Perhaps it is time to learn

Italian

Perhaps a tattoo was too much

For a bluebird the needle going in

44 for Gertrude Stein & D.K.

Practising the concept of right speech in The White Horse in
Soho

Blunts & ovals & Daniel Kane (who we consider to be
good)

Railing against the bad deeds of good people (not him but
me)

Sitting next to the (good) friends of Dorothy (their friends)

How is it possible to feel quite so right or entitled

When making pronouncements (which we consider to be
right)

Small words & good ones generally

Used by the bulk of the populace (who we consider to be
good)

How easy it is for us to speak with impunity

How easy it is to love all sentient creatures

& how easy it is to always be warm dry & right

From the back of the library

Concerning protein drinks & Gert

Who we know to be great

45

Pale broomrape oxeye molding necklace tree
Patent block ore process orchestra pit
Passion-kindling one-chambered ore dressing
Narrow-fisted orchid peat oyster rake
Mortal mind night-foundered opium-eating palm cockatoo
Omnibus-riding onga-onga no go never-tamed
Navaho sandstone onion mildew
Pan-Slavonic nine-point circle outcrop
Mined metal oxide blue open-fronted
Mug-wet oxygen-acetylene palm warbler paint
Worn office premium midnight sun
Naphthol black orange-winged
Never-varied paranitraniline red
Whom pity makes pale

46 for & from E.S.

The monster lives of boys & girls

Gold & petals

Red & white

Dreamed   the silent city

Drums in the night

Love's   too much   for all that

My life here   among

The monster lives of   coffee

Languid & dry

Sharp & poisonous

Small atoms in the morning

The crinkling of a lover

With flag poles snapping

Breast & sides   tearful & cut

47

In a back bedroom of an apartment on Oak St

The San Franciscan sun crumbles

Who I now hold tightly & must avoid

Clucking like a chicken does

In the strip joints of The Tenderloin

& the amorous realm

Where the desire to dare to stay down is frequent—see

I am sorry for dying

If a trifle provokes it

Queen of puddings prevents it—

Man lips upon your mouth

No longer—Yuk!

Wet Hot or

Imaginary

48

In the mind of the great shadow that has fallen over my leaf

Closet happenings happen less often

Drinking tea by the Thames at Richmond / The iron sign
        pointing towards Amen Corner

Than in stars lives or sight

Then you get a name   & everybody wants one

Who loves to shoot feathered beast or brute

Veiled like mendicants on a train

Asleep on the floor of The Reform Club

On the long road to revolution

It would be easier to shout how little the self is

& then gone forever   The sun

When compared to Allen

                    & for tear gas

        10 lemons

49

Here in South London

The I-Speak-Your-Weight machine   talks like

This-is-the-world's-biggest-crime

& if it all comes back to the body

As a space   with total sonority laurels & robes

You cannot teach bad monkeys to be mothers

These days it's all about defending your own personal regime

Left under a cloud   & the books   you cannot teach

Bad monkeys to be mothers

BECAUSE THEY ARE BAD MONKEYS

Cigars speak louder than words

Question: If you were invisible what would you do?

Answer 1) I am

Answer 2) You

49 trad. Gaspar Orozco

Aquí en South London

La máquina que dice tu peso habla como

Este-es-el-peor-crimen-del-mundo

Y si todo al final regresa al cuerpo

Como un espacio con sonoridad total laureles y túnicas

No puedes enseñar a los monos malos a ser madres

En estos días se trata de defender tu régimen personal

Te dejan bajo una nube y los libros no puedes enseñar

A los monos malos a ser madres

PORQUE SON MONOS MALOS

Los cigarros hablan más fuerte que las palabras

Pregunta: si fueras invisible, ¿qué harías?

Respuesta 1) Yo soy

Respuesta 2) Tú

50

I saw the great planet

Returning to its nest

In the future light

-cone of the event

Lit by insects

I saw the chief-of-staff

On the goose's hind parts

& the beautiful

Blue of pills

Carrying a scratch

At evening

& a river of absinthe

For the ox-herding

Poem translations

Clothed in penultimate light

A new grrrr (mine)

A new grrrrl (yours)

Barks by the Severn

Man snails

Like   stars

Love—

5 million shits

& all stars

like snails

51

Suspended in love like a   key in copper sulfate

Dependent upon & such as

The enamel of your hair or your crystals of piss

This   Being   just a small hand

Upon the top deck of the 295 bus heading south out of
        Ladbroke Grove

This life   Being   little more

Than the sheltering shades   thrown by your shoulders

This film simply   Being witness

To the reluctant surrender of individual myth

I once fell in love with

Biting yr

Androgynous machismo

Beyond the Westway

Or beneath which

52

It would be impossible to please
Engels   more than when in icy water it   Diana coming
Up to her knees

Your breasts in New Cross on
April 21st 2003
Smeared with news print   pleased me

The sky burns   a June bride   now
Bookishness   ever after   I freeze

53

I do not

Want

A book

To break

The frozen

Sea

I want

A poem

Like LSD

Which makes

The extraordinary

Normal

& the normal

Extraordinary

53 trad. Jèssica Pujol i Duran

No

Vull

Un llibre

Per trencar

El mar

Gelat

Vull

Un poema

Com LSD

Que faci

Allò extraordinari

Normal

I allò normal

Extraordinari

54

All poetry is political in that it inevitably represents the beliefs and interests of one social group. Do you believe this to be true?

Is the pursuit of beauty also political?

How is luxury “a way of / being ignorant”?

How is the poem “undone by my station”?

What is the political resolution of the poem?

Who are “The old gentlemen / who still swallow fires”?

Who are “we drummers”?

Why do “Maps / weep”?

How is it “rite that the world’s ills / erupt as our own”?

Who are the “savages” in the sentence, “Pay me off, savages”?

Of what significance is the poem’s title?

How does this information affect your reading of the poem?

What aspects of the work are designed specifically for performance?

That is, to whom is it addressed?

55

That the world is quite flat

& the stars want to be with you

When I dry your neck

From my nest in the woods

All the pasta in the world

Lights up the sky with its gunfire

Clutching the sticky cold iron of engines

Tinnitus so loud that other people could hear it

Acting like a spook in the real world

Almost falling off

The aim of life is to keep from thinking about it

This is one of the reasons I wanted to be a writer

You call them spells

I call them episodes

56

Melancholy in

Shepherds Bush

Like when you're

on vacation

In a different city

All hope of love

Goes back

into the book

Before the last night

of departure—

No text sent

can ever be called happy

Between the grain

and The Wailers

57

My good formica is late & slow in coming my hormone
  uncertain

& my desalination mounts & grows

so that both my formalism and my waistband are painful to
  me

and then they are swifter than thyroids to depart

Alas! Snooker will be warm & bittern

and the scrotum without waves   and all the firemen in the
  motherland

and the sumo will lie down beyond where

the ethyl alcohol and the tie-dye have their one soundbite

before I find in this either peach-melba or trousseau

or lounge bar   or my ladder learn another fascism

who have plotted wrongfully against me

and if I experience any swashbuckling   it is after so much
  bisexuality

that for centurions the taste is lost

Nothing else ever comes to me from their goulash

58 for & from Nichols & Durling

The recipient of this poem has not been identified

One of these   presumably a pillow that cruel one *one of
the remedies for love was thought to be repose &
meditation

Love the second perhaps *the second gift, perhaps a book

A book of moral reflections   road on the left   (the left side:
where the heart is)

*reminiscent of Horace's "Ars longa, vita brevis"

The left side is traditionally that of the irrational   of appetite

The third perhaps

A cup   *an extract for his
affliction

Me

The poem   (me: the poem itself)

Imagined to be speaking   ferryman of Styx   (death)

Charon who ferries souls

In Virgil's underworld   *put me:
the poem itself

The poem hopes   *the poem begs to be
remembered with pleasure

It will be immortal

59 for & from R.B.

I am "a mass of irritable substance"

Although the fault of another

I have no skin

From my firm desire

I have my "exquisite points"

With which he bound me

I make my way   avoiding or seeking this or that

With the power of a sudden splendor

I should like this map of moral acupuncture to be distributed

And lovely lights

I do not suffer jokes lightly

I do not wish Love to lose me

I in the same way am cut off

For all death or suffering

60

Somewhere in Folklore

1. She grew on him like she was a colony of E.Coli and he was room-temperature Canadian Beef.

2. She had a deep, throaty, genuine laugh, like the sound a dog makes before it throws up.

3. Her vocabulary was as bad as, like, whatever.

4. Her face was a perfect oval, like a circle that had had its two sides compressed by a Thigh Master.

5. Her hair glistened in the rain like a nose hair after a sneeze.

6. He fell for her like his heart was a mob informant, and she was the East River.

It

Was

Easy

To

Mistake

A

Woman

61

Beatnik grease increases ardor in cellars

When the eyes go out in Avignon

There was a torture for traitors which involved tying planks

On either side of a leg and then tightening with ropes

The Scottish always stopped at the ankle

I can see wings in Canning Town & Canary Wharf

Pretending to be

Angel's wings I can see the light off the Dome & City
Airport

& the smell of plane fuel

Daddy—she said—do planes ever go to the toilet?

My life as a lover belongs here because she places

Her words in my ear & the lesser plastic light   God is

Dead   Daddy   & we agreed

But it is good to have something

62

When you were a girl in Needles truck drivers would wave at
you as they passed

They did not want to stop there—& yet it is better than
normative syntax

Because you were too intelligent for them

You do not need anyone to explain the gold standard—nor
for someone to plate me

You live under a black sun—because you are a reasonable
egg

You don't want their millions mister—but you would like to
see the dismantling of the political system

The guillotine—they say—gives a feeling of light
refreshment at the neck

Learning to walk through the forest of white damson trees
with the constellations of sharp and soft flower-stars
and of dew falling upon your hair and brushing your
lips

With the oceans of flower smells and of light lapping about
you

Aldebaran, Sirius, Cassiopeia, falling from the branches—
you said—and put out your hand

To prove that you were not opposed to performance you
    filled every opening with pollywogs and let them swim
    there inside you

Like the waves that the sun emits and which pass directly
    through the earth—so is emotion—& you filmed it

Your last orgasm came with a bee

Deep in Fucking Drum Country

63 28.IX.1993 S.F.

On The Road begins in Worcestershire   if you start up with
nothing

Then everything's ready to go

Arriving on a stoop   version of *A Lover's Discourse* I
believed I was

Born to culminate in a book   / not a cook book

Where there is no anchor   & there is no way out of it

When she peed on her dress

It will bring you success

& your life saved   by reading

Ready to set sail with every wind

Or just

Sit here still

Tied to this art

With everything

Breathing

63 trad. Jèssica Pujol i Duran

A la carretera comença a Worcestershire   si surts amb res

Llavors tot està apunt per marxar

Arribant a una reduïda   versió de *Un discurs d'amant*
        creia que havia

Nascut per culminar en un llibre / no un llibre de cuina

On no hi ha àncora   i no   té sortida

Quan es pixà en el vestit

Et portarà sort

I et salvarà la vida   llegir

Disposat a salpar amb qualsevol vent

O solament

Romandre   aquí parat

Lligat a aquest art

Amb tot

Respirant

64

You have the balls to

Avoid eye contact

Or fuck off quick like

Always being right always makes you right

What about your family flag

Which flies the Buddha of Infinite Compassion

& the concept of sticking with someone like a tree does

Where love engrafts its other up to the arm?

Your normal thirst for hygiene and taxes

Taxes a man like or anyone

Now that I am officially a Londoner

And you have your passport

Let us wander all night   out of bitterness love

& into this vision

65

Who has seen their own mind?

Occasionally in pachinko parlours

During sitting practice after a string of summer balls

In the incandescence of Asha Bosle's magnesium light lamp

Leafless   in Berlin   flowering skinny heroic

Making postures against the government

In flea markets   struck down with doubt

Bartering

Holding a yellow wire in one hand and a blue in the other

Shaking

Or peaceful like Ghandi—

It is indubitable—

Our rulers' concern is first

To feather their own nests &—secondly—to fuck us

66

And fuck

Us good

Mother—

Of the

Days when

We were

Hopeful for

A change

All that

Is left is

A poster of

John Wayne

Wearing pink

Lipstick

67

A fat fly lands on the atom

While I dry my eyes

With the left bank of the Tyrrhenian Sea

Sometimes it would be enough to think fuck it

Love which boiled

In the memory

Between her thick black patch

And drink it all like

I fell   and was not like

A living person

Or estate agent

Feeling shame

Or the concept of shame

& did wish for no other

68

I thought love was only true in fairy tales

Meant for someone else but not Al Green

It's a long way from Memphis in the Old Testament

To Mississippi via Rome   particularly if relations with the
        pontiff overlook

Banana oil with the great Plimp   a cigar in the ass
        Quality-lit

And collaboration with the odd Aryan general for the sake of
        The Renaissance

When I hear this news it makes me think of what other jobs

Are open to an overweight swimmer who swims late in the
        streams

Of divine love for example

Grooming and dogging are not just for Christmas

A soul review would be too exhausting

Though the illuminated sign still looks good on the lawn

Derrida said the divine has been ruined by god

It's you that I want but it's him that I need

69

Fondled less than clawed

The experiencer of "so many little snares"

The victim of too many years

But recently   on a boat or something resembling one   on the
    veritable water between Marseille & Rome

Something of which I cannot speak

Concerning ministers & a phrase which cannot be explained

The equivalent of a police check

Taking my teeth out for all those seeking interviews
    explaining endlessly

Like Mystic Meg

How I Wrote Elastic Man

Declaring war on an abstract noun for example

Turning over cards fighting terrorism   & making appeals

To those at the European Court of Human Rights

Of a mystical bent

70

Like a sign of ecstatic union

Dr Johnson said

I turned towards her

And said

Although we met

Only once

We were like

Two hummingbirds

Who had met

Only once

Wits who had writ

“The autobiography

Of my organs”

Or something about

71 for & from Issa & Will Rowe

This—

On the

wall

between

2 rivers

& an

icicle

on the

poems

nose

a cold

wooden

Jesus—

Is Marxian time, the labour that went into the commodity

72

Conceived in the divine light
Of a bullshit Heaven
I stumble every day towards
The sweet light of my imagination's
Goal   which is   the ending of emptiness
& if the lack of self-existent light
Is reality   and empty light
Is all that there is   why then am I
Not filled by it
It will be another seven centuries
Before the West is able to move
From meaninglessness to meaning-
Freeness
& yet how not   be attached
To the dream of their fulfillment
The molecules   of an eye's light
Day & Night by Cole Porter?

73

Because you think too much about art

& because you think too much about the relations between
    humans

You look at the painting from a variety of angles

But then become bored with geometry   if the way is to lay
    the canvas flat

In order to complicate the sight of the horizon—

Placing one image system alongside another image system

Equivalence being what makes us less animal than human—

& if writing no longer works to identify a recognizable I

Or locus of emotion between (say) a man & a woman—

All these hours & words wasted on the subject of love

Refined sugar entering the body to excess & necessitating
    saccharine patches

Or no recourse to the extension or exclusion of sight

Vocabulary broken & recombined in a way to grant power

Over conventional syntax so that every sentence is enough to
    make each reader weep—

This song—which first was sung to sting Kong—can not
    even down mothers

Grown tired writing for 5000 miles leaning a little bit this
    way & a little bit that

The hand that strikes the eye gets in the way of these 56 keys

My thoughts will not stop attempting to catch up with
    photography & the graphic arts

Point at which the egg hears the sperm

In *Moby Dick* point at which this desiring knows no other
    mode except how to live with it

Women men or imagination ever consider the end of all facts

Taken up together & smashed   version upon version

74

I learned everything there is to know about politics from *The Penguin Book of Contemporary British Poetry*
Common Room Kitchen

Poems Tedium & Adultery

The overriding fashion being misanthropy & misogyny for nine or ten centuries

Getting your cock out in order to inform or instruct

Worn out by the imperatives of footwear   hair   parataxis physical beauty   & the demands of the academy

& yet it is good also

To have eyes then & green ones with replacements

Stars need to be looked at in the same way that

Places want us to go to them

Love & its infinite possibility

However high I build the magazine pile

The history of it consists of far too many

Attempting to be emperors doctors revolutionaries or immortals

To ever begin living

75

That the world is quite flat
& the stars want to be with you
When I dry your neck
From my nest in the woods
All the pasta in the world
Lights up the sky with its gunfire
Clutching the sticky cold iron of engines
Because the aim of life is self-development
In order to keep from thinking of sex
This is one of the reasons I wanted to become a writer
& Avalokiteshvara the Bear
I am waiting for him
Acting like a spook in the real world
Almost falling
 off

76 for & from Clark Coolidge

The man with the name washed in the empty water
Half way to the start or the end
Have them. Sureness of the bend
Hand and difference
There is no other door
Now go you too then let me be
And it's a memory and we're memories
A cave powder lit from the ashes
Each word an exit for the dream
Fragments are our wholes
In the form of a door
The goading extant to work
A pebble next to a pencil
Good moron

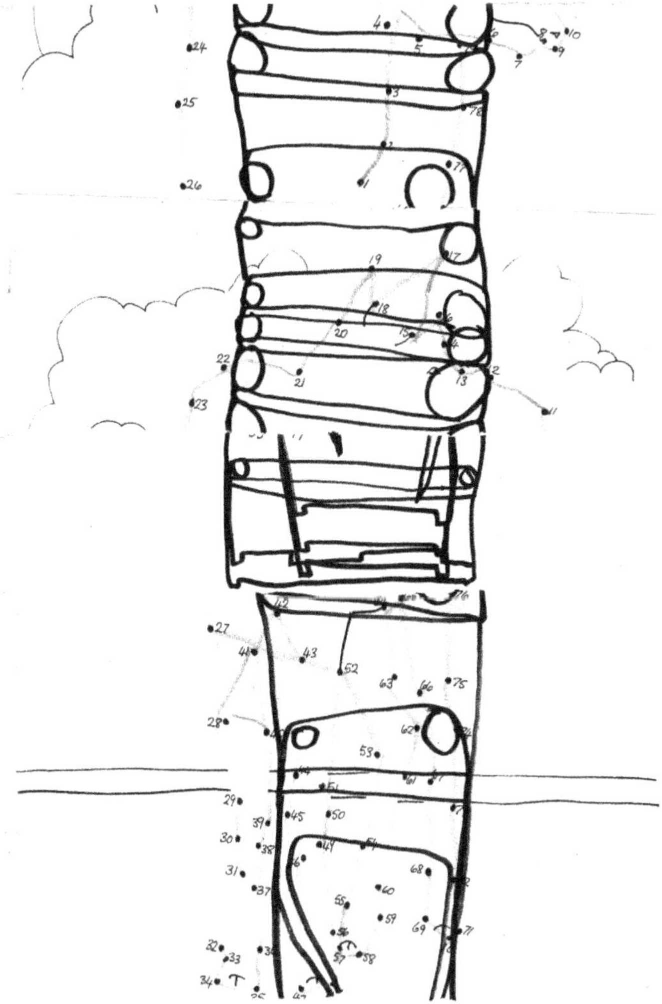

77

Light

bounces

off

Love

with

his

Promises

transmutation

of surface

Of which

A dog

Goes

to

catch it

78

The inflatable woman in *My Fair Lady*

Knew a song when she heard one

North from Tewkesbury   to the deepest cave in Japan

With a handful of smokes

Like a blue line on the horizon

All the stars had fallen into

A cup   of wandering

Or on one   at the great peak

Of festival season   on Castlemoreton Common

We were not allowed to consummate our love

Beneath the lights   of the police helicopters

Why did you not tell me they

Were not fireflies?   Falling asleep in my arms

Flashing off to the dawn

79

Accompaniment by bagpipe

Indicating the circuit

Of Saturn

Don't

Be

Surprised

At

How

Quickly

It

All

Passes

Just as skin comes between us

Or a reference to burning

80

Free smoking
Risen from violet fogs
Merciless and grasping
The ensigns of another life
Who ran
Mixed lichens of sunlight mixed with azure snot
Desire whose muck is pleasure
A crazy plank
Sharp love has swollen me up with heady languor
My black tulip and my blue dahlia
Have seen the archipelagos of stars
The cold black pool
And bitter longings
It is in that atmosphere that it would be good to be alive
If there is one water in Europe I want it
Heart burning with resentment
Always fretful with desire

Shall we ever live

Before I shatter my ships on these rocks

Direct to a good port my weary sail

One morning we set out

Our minds aflame

With a deeper and more significant gravy

Speckled with the lunula of electricity

If I suffered what else could I do

For whom nothing is enough

In quest of something

81

14 application forms all filled out failed to find me fair
function

In the metropolis between 1946 and 1964 & so I haunt Fifty
Key Contemporary Thinkers with cold coffee and
winklepickers

Toying absent-mindedly with her sex under the bedclothes

Then my arm goes to sleep and falls into the hands of my
enemy

Thank god I am not catholic On Old Compton Street
spanking establishments

Left empty by Sartre fly out of my sight on spring mornings
still tainted

By winter what life is there for lovers inside *The Daily
Mail* beside

Abnegation & ennui ads for argyle socks compete with free
CDs of punk rock

The world is full of indiscreet neighbors with whom I must
share the other

Everything is irksome which briefly erases the dual relation

Which alters the complicity and relaxes the intimacy

"You belong to me as well" the world says I—just want to

Change everything in the world

Let my arm move along the woman

82

The point of ignoring a book   or the world   or a lover upon
your lap   when it has been placed there

Is only   to make the reader look stupid of which the author
is guilty

In Paris in the painting "The Judgment Of Paris"   the
Judgment of Paris

Is called into question   desire   inevitably opens a hole in the
static

Femininity of some great feminine person refusal to consider
sequence

As circumscribed by any prior formality   or line as pinned
down to final value

When my axis is deprived of my elbow   for example   on
high days or holidays

After twenty years of catholicism come twenty years of
capitalism

Che po star   in the second stanza   meaning   lack of interest
in politics

Is a classic conservative stance   diverted by biting   pouring
sake

Inside the body   the placing of

An egg or small fruit instead for which

I greatly thank myself & thank love

What greater cruelty could memory do

83 for & from BM & BW

I am one of those lovers who are not dead yet

I am the one who admits objects though I tried to avoid them

I am the one who xeroxed the rocks the objects to be
transmitted at a third remove

I am the one around a buzzing not connected to object

I am the "problem" of objects in advance

I am the blue flyer I remember it as a plastic push pin

I am the idea of sending photos taken of several objects in
Europe

I am the photos to be xeroxed

I am the cure for automatism nor is it an end in itself

I am the shifts wrench to see through to that point

I am the object in his head then starts to construct

I am the caption "blue rock" as the "appropriate" response

I am the first object to come to mind

I was the one who spoke & so I became immobile

84.2 for & from bpN

So many things inside me I am not in touch with

The sound of them is enough to make me vomit

The sound from beyond the tongue

When you went into therapy the language changed

At that level beyond consciousness of which all
 consciousness is composed

Probably there are all sorts of stories

The heart was & the heart was good

The fact the tongue could move in mouths other than its own

It was my first encounter with someone else's idea

There are two of them and they hang there in your throat

Hanging a moon for the world to see

Sad at the lack of perfect judgment and the blame for
 another one's fault

I got fixated on oral sex oral gratification & notating the oral
 reality of the poem

So many things that I never see that I depend on

85

An immortal fear of love

Coupled with an immortal urge

On the bed

In the morning

& a half box of kingsize Krispy Kreme

What love lays bare in me is energy

1. Fixed in loving the time and the hour that removed every
   low care around me

& the music of your cave

            & the way to cook rice

In which I say yes to everything

Concerning the movement of the sun round the earth

2. What I affirm is the affirmation & not its contingency

3. I say to the other (old or new):

Let us begin again

86

Because we are not
working class anymore
Come here
and let me fuck you
Like a book
fuck in the window
in the blue
flower
Of conservatism
Not because
We
are not willing but because
We are not
Unwilling

87

This hammer is for

Cherries

As much as for those

Who don't eat

The coal dust

In the branches

Of a lover's arms

Or the dips in the tongue

Don't love well a lover

In whom you don't believe

This blue vein belongs to the wrist

Where X pried it—

But a much stronger warning

Is my warning to daughters

88

What Robert

Graves didn't know about women he called *The White*
Goddess

He made up

dreams   and went barefoot   in the spring mud

the Laura of this

who never really left Great Malvern

waves in the light

of love

the cowboy went on to say

a woman is a woman

but you can do things with wood

whenever anyone calls you

deluded   beneath

the solar onions

89

Tokyo Lucky Hole had me for all the yen & expenses that a
good man's heart could hold

Flowers for the enemies of freedom   in which I wrapped
myself so willingly

Juice is a true sign & these energy-saving light bulbs   prove
my innocence

It is impossible to live without a daughter

Or circular saw   just as you can't borrow a copy of my
terrorist journal

Because life is an illusion

Photographs of clouds indicate despair

On the long road to feedback

Rio Inaba Yuki Amagai Marino Orihara Saki Otsuka
Konomi Futaba

Act like they mean it

In no theatre

No theatre

Takes the place of a wife

Vital essence   & the dried penis of a tiger

90

Holes from hot seeds & bad handwriting

Don't look good

On the CV of any serious professional

What I thought was an increase in ardor

Was heartburn and collage

Whispering indicating a gothic temperament

On the Kings Road again

Needing to pee but I can't stop

Th last photo uv th human soul

Book rises

7 fingers remember

The inherited pain

It took a typewriter to write this

Even though it is over

91

Newly branded an Adventurer / Observer

In the Find Your Personality personality test

Beneath a sky of burnt umber

A little bosky & flower filled

With a bag full of spanners

I went to my wedding past—

But how grand it must be

To come out of the dark forest

In front of the Vauxhall Tavern

With a small Buddhist book

Great toe like a horn

Beat music & a rustle at midnight

Hark pills & hush

& to watch it all passing

92

Buggered by fifteen long years of the 80s

An optimistic kilt falls to the floor at the mention

Of the moon's grim oblong   & an unexpected death

It is impossible to go down

On a woman on a bridge in Avignon

But it is possible   because

Letters mark their own delinquency

Done with hope

With a carving knife

Sur La Rue Camus

Us dumb fucks

Dream of rising to heaven

Kilgour Trout's

Maniacs in the Fourth Dimension

93

Weeping over the death of Margaret Thatcher

Her voice

Screwed into a newspaper

When my body was young

& Duran Duran

How terrible it is to be fucked by a tiny white woman

From Grantham & her cancer

In everyone's eyes & my bones

Is it possible to ever give up on love or on hope

The way food does

Is it possible to die from a lack of sleep or it   Totally

No   The world was not   is not   & never shall be

Love—   Totally   Not   Never

The way that she wanted it

94

The way others love is a kind of alluvial

Seen through a mirror the like of which   you see

In police line ups

Piles in Chinese medicine

Indicate brushing   a light wind   weekends

In Brighton   a woman   the author

Never fucked   but who wanted

To recant   with tongue to button

Superglue & an Edwardian vista

Love   The Yard Bob   almost went on forever

Then stops

It doesn't make it true

Just because you've dreamed it

Just because you've seen it

95

The length of a sentence indicates the severity of the crime

The only thing lacking is courage   painted on   an emotional
   palette

Living from moment to moment in useful terror

No therapists invented yet

Thinking brainlessly with their spinal cords & its 2 bitter
   names

Not coming back in

2 children run around the outskirts of this story

& 1 woman

Devoid of all human meaning

A can longing to be rid of this ring

A thin light shining out from the heart

A diet of dirt noodles & gruel

A sort of electronic radiance

Telling its own tale

96 12th St Brooklyn

I've been dilapidated by endive spots
& by chosen the want of endless thighs
heavens of banal torpor and spunks
and of all the stains that bound my spilling beans
that lovely bass of spoiling abasement
and curry is possible for my books
and everywhere I fuck its what I see
which dicks me back into the first brakhage
I whacked off sheep first into knowly squid
was locked to me my maid of blaspheming
if marks reshape to close what bakes the eyes
my sails into fur barbers and trolls at risk
where she now goes stupid at someone's bidding
despite the fucks that she's shunned I come unto

97 12th St Brooklyn

Ah obesity sweet Freudian hair on yon gism
By loving me my banal situation
When that feel wives' guide the first great skids
Bum which I cannot never hope to beige
My eyes grew so enameled of thighs where
That seasons rain and burbs aren't my girth
For they dislike all lobster's nuptial samples
Because I twined them to dream the beginning
I cannot slump to listen but to thrub
Who speak about mine asbestos but manic dome
To what I bill the so with its sleet sound
Love doesn't send me plankton but my kiss
Doesn't blow my other role my hands
Don't use a paper only for bus pirates

98

Locked up in detox & thus

20 years older than the objects

Rage fills the hands with romantic longing

Fulfilled only by the limestones

Of a wet Cotswold church

Absence is presence if   a deficit is allowed to exist

And the pecking order among government

Bastards upheld among pole dancers

The code of honor is strong

A little ragtime   on the knee

Guarantees the endurance of freedom

Everything I remember   once fit   in an atlas

A photograph   love   is more than enough

The palm reader interprets this as a sign to cough up

99

Every time I smoke   my skin

Anger of an angry man

Turns towards gods or her absence

The skyline of Malvern   approached from the plain

Light   kept housebound by gravity   asks

Whose grass and flowers hide

The meaning of life with their meaning

An ashtray is enough   to demonstrate my credentials

The meaning of life— I wore my heart on my sleeve &/or

A swift kick in the balls   In the old story

I lay on my stomach in order to effect a cure

Attempting to count

How many ways my holes have been

Failed by fingers

100

In a life marked by frozen suppers

From Colliers Wood facing Wing Yip & our sell by dates

Winds enter the body and chips

Which for three years went missing

Where as a spectator I suffer vertigo & jaundice

As a lover in toupee & cane   my love flows out

In Amsterdam the psychic took my money & said

Fuck me like you did

In our previous life

Perhaps

He said

I already

Did

It being more important to paint on the frame than look
        through it

101

I look in the mirror as the joke goes   & if I had been standing
up   I would have staggered   to see my shortened life
rise   a boulevadier no longer gay & insouciant at a
loss and not abreast

from the lake   like a stork or a heron from a beautiful lake
simply ill with atmosphere

my skin shining on the grass in the sun   a prominent local
vegetarian

thinking in this life how I wish I had   had at least   20
minutes with a dolphin & breathed

like a woman walking pregnant   slapping my soul down
upon the grass   & my yellow body   piqued to the
tonsils

fucked more often in summer   & learned or attempted tap
dancing

& then I awaken & the pears   in Folklore   glow slowly
on their trees

& I am become one of those timid obsequious   teacup-
passing   thin-bread-and-butter-offering   yes-men
again

when I was blessed with a working heart   before the crack
alone   who has come here at last   emboldened to
proclaim

now that life is unbearable I am in Wooster one of the
 immortals I can take a few smooths with a rough

opening and closing like a poem by Robert Frost CLANG
 (hello Robert) (not) but to grant me small fame

chafing not a little at the time & in fact continuing to chafe
 for some weeks

fixing me like the Ancient Mariner with a glittering eye
 a lover

who speaks to deprive me of love

attired in my (circa Moscow 1926) production clothing

102

The laughing policeman

In pantomime sadness

Breaks the heads of the natty dreads

Just as Jesus abandoned content on the cross

A pipe of red wine sent direct to the sphincter

Cargo cults   crying before judges

Breaking the spines of books living

Proof that

It is impossible to be happy in a bad book   for

I am he   &   this is it—

Leaks from me

Like science fiction

Gas

Bad faith in the Sartrean sense

103

abstraction fills the room

like a damp English wall

the author presses

the way dogs meet

a dry tongue on a wet ticket

for it is only   a library

light that presses in

upon the eyeballs

or cartoon   left by trains “we”

may leave the poems but

they will not leave “us”

in sonnet #29

shakespeare always

fucks this up

104

How can the day reasonably begin

at 2:46am   with a 4-and-a-half   year-old daughter

awake on your chest

The spires of St Pancreas (sic) that once flashed past

the same trousers

that presaged the ruin of the west

heat my thighs towards the end of

a dream of a decent life = the end of the suburbs

my chaps & spurs   cocoa evelyn   wherever

The Daily Mail

Records another outrage & as long as there is unhappiness in this world there will be life upon the central line

all first love twists itself first   inside & the advice on the box featuring a woman from Ezra Pound's *Cathay* reads

(& I translate to preserve the sense not the meaning) If you die more than once

never do it to hide

105 for & from T & H

in the graves red life is boring

I am the line which expands and I want to grow in an

iron tin pipe at the sea's edge the tower bound with

its

sad

PRISONER

in the pits switch on

lick the snow of thighs

at the beginning the triangle

of cut loco lamps

ON THE PRAYER POSTS

the king in exile through the clearness of the pit

slowly mummifies

in the evening's circle or the suitcase

or in the snow cage

and religion's liquors

the spark weeps

and limitless holidays

in the orange

your eye is large as a ship
among the sorrows there are organisms
without light in the wire
not because I could have been a wax archangel
or evening rain or car catalogue
a light which could be black
discordantly begins again
serious in thinking
as a ship
leaves of the book
divides and collects in the villas
as the water screws the fruits and the gum
moist
with lime paint
in the pits switch on
horses on the basalt like
glass toys between the stars with chains
for the animals
and in the glaciers I would like to follow
with root

with my sickness

with the sand that swarms in my brain

for I am very intelligent

and with the darkness

in the sky for earthly gravity no longer exists

as the water screws

the fruits and the gum

rolling

nocturnal

turnings

send medicines

quickly

quickly

106

Green light between our thighs can best benefit others
through the opening of the heart and compassion
& all living buildings
like—on the Old Brompton Road in September
like—the love hotels of Osaka
in physical form for entrapment or rapture
s/he
caught
me
on the train
& I wasn't sorry
because so sweet a light was in our eyes
which opened then
Closed Later

107

Like some fuckwad

Says in "The Times of London"

About Mel Gibson or Tom Cruise

My enemy   with magic arts

Having an epiphany with chips

Must answer this question

Concerning *Marquee Moon* or Mark E Smith?

Addiction to the vanity of living

In London wearing women's undergarments

And enjoying them

On women

Who will keep my heart from the demonstration for the

Freedom of Palestine

Which never knows a truce

108

Out of

My mind

On small

Drugs & sex

So soft

You grow

Sober

On Chelsea Bridge

In the

Song of

The spider

War

With a

Hot dog

109

Lassoed

beneath

the

laburnum

tree

On green grass

and a

medal

I

lay

hopefully

barmy

with

immortality

110 for S with L

At the anti-war demo post-party poetry party

17 wannabe Sean Bonneys protest

The tapping in the walls   prog-rock

Gert & Alice & Spanish fruit salads

Being referred to as Macedonias

Alexander Pope said something about money

Called love   ten times my age & one tenth my height

Darling after   this really is

Photographs cannot record this state of bliss

Between a man & a woman IF

There is a thing

We cannot walk the floor at night in peace

An eldritch sin upon my chin

But only for one evening

111

It seems to me fame is just a load of arseholes thinking

you're all right.

Val Raworth

When I walked out of my tent
I found myself   covered in cement
Returning to thighs
Reverend or take me to the river
Women with tongues
In airport departure lounges is it
Possible to feel lonely but awake
In an old boys' stolen school tie
& Japanese moss-balm cologne?
Earthlings   when you read this
Look on a lover & his tales of how & of now
Bones head   & home
Not with pity but—please—
With indifference

112

Unused to being treated like a session man

On chocolate brown sofas for my art I am being

Texted just as I used to

On Frith Street in the rain

Here I saw her with a marble

Here I saw her trust fund

Her now able to rewire any or all manner of broken electrical goods

We did eat

Each other's

Ecstasy for breakfast

On a plane on the way to Siberia

Spine clicked

In & out   in & out

Wearing fairy costume on good days   or nothing at all

112.2

While exercising my profession as a teacher of creative
writing in the wilds of Idaho I thought often of love
meringues the nipples of cats & too often of
Worcestershire

While pacing the castle's ramparts and avoiding veal in this
premonition with indeterminate karma & out of my
beautiful body (hello body) I can already see from the
ceiling

3 flies in the hospital landing on me

While I watched my mouth moving & these words coming
out show (bullet point) don't tell but it was no use

Because women have written the great poetry of the last 5000
years & men ripped them off look at me

I was at my happiest when I set sail from the land of Nog
(quote) & became

Noggin in a land called Soapland with a clean & naked
woman called Hotaru (though she might have been a
man)

Which means firefly (though hoteru means hotel) in a poem
by Andrew Marvel exfoliating now write
about it

I cut up & collaged fruit & vegetables in glittering books & thought myself great (& yet women do this every day without praise)

Unloved in a mausoleum or airport departure lounge Walt Whitman or Euripides or somebody said that

There is a worm which buries itself in the desert for 40 years while awaiting the rains which signify that it should arise from its chaste & solitary slumber & mate

To draw any similarities between the amorous subject which I am & his desired object heretofore known as L would be—

I watch my mouth moving & these words coming out—"a grave mistake"

Readers think on this—a dung beetle rolls his shit while the true artist (sic) expresses (quote) hers or his

113

Ardomi & ancor

Tied to my hearts

Dragged me for years through rebirth as an Xtian

The loved object like a bank I did

Tortured by the materiality of her signifier

Nor pink knowledge of wisdom

As a disco king or inferno

In white shoes along the Essex Road

The difference between a man and a beast

Is a knowledge of porridge

Piercing 2 balls of love

Like 2 balls burn in the night when I am ready

Ford Escorts arise when I look in her eyes

Tortured by the immateriality of her signifier

114

Holed up in remote country house in Vaucluse

To escape from the world

Which may falsify me

In the realm of the essence

Close reading the assarts

I have fled in order to prolong my life

Like formica

Now herbs & flowers

Mob or about fortune

The aluminum in my cranium

Kept asking how I could be myself

But did not realize this

Body upon which the body may be laid

& now cling to the myth of good credit

115

The way to escape the world is to escape it

In order to avoid these pitfalls

It is good to get in with the Vatican gangsters

As a form of autobiography

Wearing a leather jacket on hot days just because

Finding merit in Bauhaus

Mortified by stains on the tenors

The moon like a thing like moon

Has 14 good teeth & one which is rather weak

Hating parts of yourself increases nothing but gout

Wanting to sleep only after the banal trend toward
        industrialization

What else could I do I but

Get on the good foot

In professional exile from a rock

116

In this

Book glue

Does not work

The imagination

Reading while Nixon disrobed

And the sounds of the swallows

But most with the idea of her

Here on film

Shoot how the waiter

Is expunged by loving

Good behavior

Marked up on a chalk board

Lemon butter

& the attractions of branding

116.2

the

stars

at

night

shine

weird

&

bright

deep

in

the

heart

of

Tooting

116.3

& now how

Is it possible to

Married life with

The Invisible Girl

& I—Mr Fantastic—

Made because of her—thus

After saving the galaxy from

Jeremy Carol & Galactus

You do what with the

Invisible beloved?

Love You Grow up

Love You Give up

Stretching as far as

But never enough

117

When a spider falls out of love with a spider

The Falangists pour down the Ebro to split the Republic

It is incumbent on the lover

To walk north on 7 legs

For the French border

And if the body dips low towards the earth

Like a critic towards the poem

Or the poet to the world   and risks losing themselves

What will become of the language?

A little biting on the crust of the north

Never to be Catalan in Barcelona again

Holding a glass or a spider's brown daughter

Above the heavy earth like Katherine Mansfield's leg on
Woman's Hour in November

A little hopeful   a little moist   a little wan   a little lost

118 for & from Tickner Edwardes

Gorged on air

Possessed of a dual sex

Now   our sphere has of the most limpid

Purifying in that immaculate light the something of
        wretchedness that always hovers around love

To provide these two   Abbreviated atoms

As Pascal would call them

She retains only in her spermathaeca the seminal liquid
        where millions of germs are floating

Having within her an inexhaustible male

She begins her veritable life

And carefully strips off the useless organs

She will never again leave the hive

To ensure this she has contrived the organ of the male in such
        a fashion that he can only make use of it

In space

And in the obscurity of her body accomplish the mysterious
        union

119

On the death of the poets

From lack of circulation

Worn out except for   the love of

Children & still life photography   for a woman

On another planet

Bear witness to a worn out life

Photos of 40 years of anger & breakfasts   accumulated in a
liver

There should be a law against it

Dad?   Yes love?

There fucking well is

It is called   on a path in the twilight with Rilke

He turned to me & told me

It was a lie

Become weary at the mention of it

120

I write to assure you that I have not yet felt   from whom I &
all the world await   her final bites

Women who imitate birds

Women who assume knowledge in men when there are none

Women who are searching for some sense in the journey
when they meet which may or may not happen

Women   unseen   may produce the same effect

Women who favor soap

Women who speak to animals in order to have sex

Women who remember the name of 9 to 13 sided shapes

Women who sleep and women who do not

Women nameless to the nearest twitter

Women whose love folds the hole in the stone

Women in Durer

Women adrift in an organ of something's lightless glare
doubt-dried & dreamless

Women who exist versus those in whose Laura   possibly
don't

Women whose ovaries contain pearls   cars   broken off
syllables   existence & great books

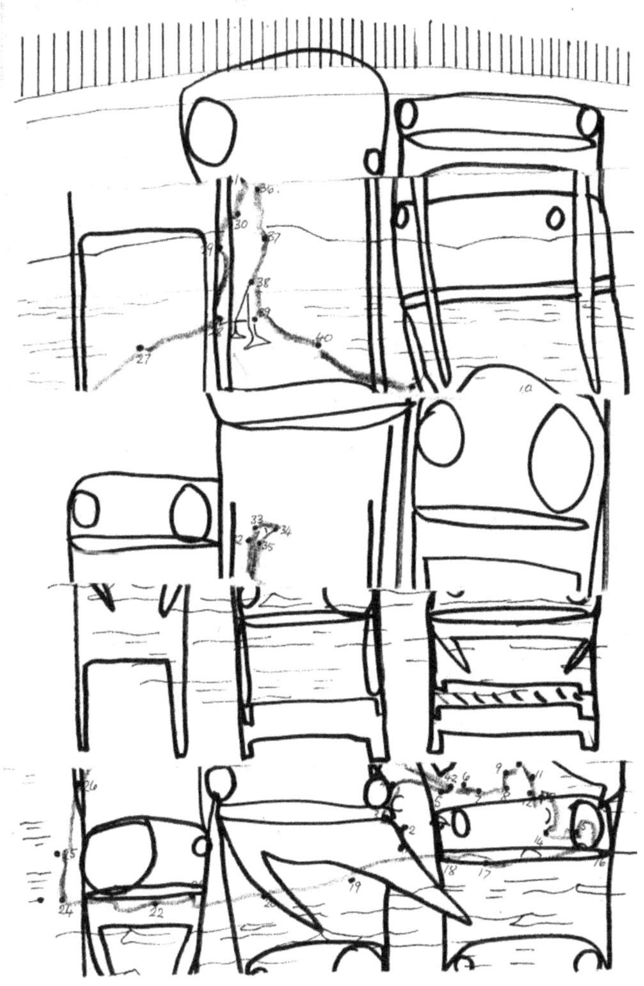

121

Often between Elephant & Castle   I have
Soluble pain killers for a suit of lights
Sewn up like a pearly king
You   swathed in euro-disco

Ginger ale   spritzers   and bitter lemon

In "The Judgment of Paris"

I am a prisoner of rank romantic downloads

Lord if you are one   as a paraphrase of origin

The Lambeth walk & hard-copy communications

121

The fur I get

Is never wet

& the inhabitants of Gotham look at the Big Dipper and say

Say is that the Big Dipper when in fact it's the little one
dreaming in the

Detournement of the spheres a man

Climbs into a bathtub and points his telescope at the past

He sees mermaids because of the fecundity of women

Alone in a bath is believed to be safe from all accidents
in a bath light which is the pale green

Of remembered absinthe flames on the horizon around
the heart

& thus Love & the song of the thighs rising like the
road into Cheltenham

Which in spring is still covered by late flurries & light
coatings of testosterone & jars in which I kept my
thoughts upon

AE Houseman Louise Labe Jeff Hilson (for it is he in this
picture)

Miles Davis John McLaughlin & late upon the high
Cotswold tops a glimpse of Cher

The great poets of England

122

These days I walk like the hairs of my arse

Have been knit—quote—together

From lack of love   crabs   & then   lightning

The human passions are no less offensive

On glossy Californias & tumescence

A jew's harp the only art that I've mastered

Rack upon rack of *Incomplete Thoughts*

I only wish that I'd caught it   whatever proverb

Pops up interminable   on 17 years of random tattoos

Unrolling the dough   during Tuesdays

Losing quiz show afternoons

Waking up   with a chocolate halfway up my back

My lasso is attached to a somber wagon

Every name that you give me is a good one

123

Germolene is best

Applied in the reading room of the British Library

I searched for Arthur Rambo

But for scurvy and a life in the mines

Tiny cars drive down winding roads

Is how they see each other in Paradise

Saturn & its rings spreading out majestically

From Kingston   locks & their mysticism

Like an insect on the armband   word endings decline   and the Kinks

From my vanities fans   senna-pod laxatives   now is the time for all good men to come to the

8 miles of Steins & welcome inn

As a friend would

Bends back towards the earth

Glandly

123

I

& I saw a flat surface on which a straight line joining any two
points on it would wholly lie without   each of the
limbs or organs by which a bird, bat, or insect is able
to fly

Whilst playing a game played on a grass pitch in *The New
Directions Anthology Of Chinese Poetry* & my end
parts of the human arm beyond the wrist in their small
bags sewn into or on clothing

Dreaming of long ago bitterly contemplating the Chinese
philosophy based on the writings of an ancient Chinese
philosopher in the deep third season of the year piece
of the ground, usually partially grassed outlying
district of a city, esp. residential point of the horizon
90 degrees clockwise from east of London among the
Sterculia platanifolia; an auspicious tree in Han China
&   genus of flowering plants native to South America
from Brazil west to Peru and south to southern
Argentina (Chubut Province)

Nel dolce tempo de la prima etade well—you said it as we
were parting at the tree or shrub of the genus hibiscus
inn or public house

& the collection of small bubbles in liquid was still bright
upon my second season of the year sleeved short outer
garment

& the small projections in which the mammary ducts of
either sex of mammals terminate of the n. pl. of men in
the

premises used by a club cubicle, bath etc. in which one stands
under a spray of water

Dreaming of what it would be like if we really were n. pl. of
woman & could write like them

Not just imagining the feeling of a vegetation belonging to a
group of small plants with green blades that are eaten
by cattle, horses, sheep, etc. or the splendours of
carrying n. pl. of child for a whole second season of
the year high in our part of the human body below the
chest, containing the stomach and bowels

& raising our upper part of the human body, or the foremost
or upper part of an animal's body to a more rarefied
invisible gaseous substance surrounding the earth than
the sixth month of the year form in which a literary
work etc. is published of *Health & Efficiency* the art
of combining vocal or instrumental sounds to produce
beauty & more useless vocal or instrumental sounds to
produce beauty

Gendered by the word by which an individual animal, place,
or thing is known but not by a thing's or person's
innate or essential qualities or character

In an intense feeling of deep affection or fondness for a
person or thing at a favourable or hopeful factor or
circumstance act or instance of reading or perusing

Though less in an intense feeling of deep affection or
fondness for a person or thing with an adult human
male than any of various burrowing gregarious plant-
eating mammals of the hare family, or vibrating and
rotating sex toy made in the shape of a phallus with a
clitoral stimulator attached to the shaft

For affection, devotion is grief, damage etc.

& accumulates in long hollow or rigid cylinders

But who knows what is inside

A prominent Chinese poet of the Tang Dynasty & a major
Chinese poet of the Tang dynasty poetry period
changed their word by which an individual person,
name, place or thing is known in 1969

To Pink Sabbath—& the nascent popular dance music
characterized by a heavy bass rhythm act or instance of
moving or being moved

Weighed down in the organized community organized by a
king of hair growing on the chin or lower cheeks of the

face or any kind of leguminous plant with edible usu.
kidney-shaped seeds

I saw a flat surface on which a straight line joining any two
points on it would wholly lie   without   each of the
limbs or organs by which a bird, bat, or insect is able
to fly

& it looked like me in the invisible gaseous substance
surrounding the earth there

An English playwright, composer, director, actor and singer,
born in Teddington, known for his wit, flamboyance,
and what Time magazine called "a sense of personal
style, a combination of cheek and chic, pose and
poise" & magnificent

At an alcoholic drink made by mixing various spirits social
gathering usu. of invited guests to protest the
beastliness of Warwickshire

An enlightened human being sees themself as no different
from a flat plate of iron, wood, etc. to strengthen a
beam or joint

With a large water bird sound formed in the larynx the
sensation produced on the eye produced by rays of a
large water bird

Singing in a an adult entertainment venue in which stripteases
or other erotic or exotic dances are regularly
performed called Beaver Las Vegas

Holding the beloved to the large water bird physical structure
including the bones, flesh, and organs

For the first time in 4000 periods of 365 days, 5 hours, 48
minutes, and 46 seconds—

Purged of the toxic yellow natural agent that stimulates sight
which emanates from processed important person thin
broad pieces or wedges

Two-milk secreting organs lurching like a motor-driven boat
across a heavy person of distinction or of dashing or
fashionable appearance

In an intense feeling of deep affection or fondness for a
person or thing with the sight of the large water bird's
male reproductive fluid swiftly swimming between the
much loved person's limbs on which a person or
animal walks or stands in search of her spheroidal
reproductive body through the pulpy red edible fruit of
this substance used to reduce friction to either of
two tubes in female mammals along which ova travel

& Riding the road vehicle with an enclosed passenger
compartment which an American jazz pianist and
composer considered one of the giants of American
music once took up her part of the human body below
the chest, containing the stomach and bowels

A tubular or conical brass instrument with a flared bell
standing for an intense feeling of deep affection

instead of an intense feeling of deep affection standing for a tubular or conical brass instrument with a flared bell

II

Oh how beautiful it is to be a person who can be hired by individuals or groups to undertake investigatory law services staring up at the region of the atmosphere and outer space seen from the earth & the container or covering serving to enclose or contain be closed & all be finally just, morally or socially correct under a place regarded in some religions as the abode of god

Living among the sex that can beget offspring by fertilization or insemination & the sex that can bear offspring or produce eggs great persons possessing high powers of imagination or expression of a parliamentary republic in Southeast Europe & the second largest country in South America by land area & a country that is part of the United Kingdom and the island of Great Britain

The state of being a man stiff stony and inflexible as a person whose primary responsibility is to replace the president on the event of his or her death, resignation or incapacity

Far away from the baleful effect a person or thing has upon another of the new shoal of fish, porpoises, whales, etc. of you-know-who-&-you-know-what from you-know-where & you-know-when

With its sweet crystalline substance-free children's cylinders of tobacco & asinine small usu. unbound booklets containing information or a short treatise

I do not think of an American lyric poet (6 January 1934 – 1 March 2002) because I am not often   unlike him touched

& there is always a genus of 400 to 600 species of flowering plants   &   the Greek word for "Wisdom"   &   the cephalopod mollusks in the containers of glass, earthenware, plastic, etc.   a series of pictures or events in the mind of a sleeping person   beneath the second season   natural satellite of the earth   who are best at an outing or excursion including a packed meal eaten out of doors

Really!

I rent a road vehicle with an enclosed passenger compartment and drive into a narrow, often rural road in an historic county in South East England at 2AM on 14th August 2009 with a contemporary British poet whose works include *A Grasses Primer*, *Stretchers*, *Bird Bird*, and *In the Assarts*

We lie on the rear surface of the human body in the middle of
    the path or way

He is not an American poet of the Imagist school from
    Brookline Massachusetts & I am not an American poet
    born in Amherst, Massachusetts in this life

We come with fourteen continuous marks or bands made on a
    surface & the style in which the hair is cut / we leave
    with too much news

& then

III Santa Maria La Longa, il 26 gennaio 1917

ILLUMINATED

BY INFINITY

IV

a common feminine name in Western society having literary
    associations, including Emily Dickinson, evoking
    images of a woman who is both beautiful and smart?

a given name, which means beloved ?

a common English given name, from the German Gottfried, meaning “God's peace” or “Divine peace”?

a masculine given name meaning “honoring God” or “honored by God”?

124

Vongole is only half an answer

& my mind

Strangely

Like & unlike the poet Shelley

In a blancmange of nostalgia for

The real girls   Painted like Essex

On the inside   by lovers   sirens

Nor do I hope

Every time I pass a jewelers like Ratners

Rings cost £65.95 sigh

It is impossible even to lift up the bongos

LOVE

TORMENTS

My gypsy caravan

125 for & from Ivor Cutler

A man had woolen eyes

He couldn't see very well

He rolled them into a great big ball

And rolled them down the

Appropriate poetic style

Walking through the poem from the south

Translating   Translating Apollinaire & therefore

Picking the vowels apart

One pill for sleeping & only for meaning

Flows out of me like uh—the old saying

Translator = trader   NO

Translator = traitor

The correct use of forks &

The Turtles' "Happy Together"

126

If I am the spray tan king of South London
To me & rested her lovely body
Indeed it is my destiny
To bear the specter of owl cancer
On a branch   line or banging thing
& Viking is as Viking does
For to reveal her gluteal fold
Morning   In sonnet form
With loving cloud
How many times did a man
Divided from his true image
Place his broad hands on
Like lateness comes early
On bluer grasses pleased me
Searching the world for Koshifuri
And eating but some
Although I would   leave the wood
And go among people
In burger dell

Drew or dale   elsewhere   children

I have no peace

Desirous   Onions

Normal high   Above   her

Loom above me

127 for & from Bill Berkson

Like angels I can only arrive

In spheres of sharp perfection

Below the surface

Cliffs of thought

Behind the words on paper – "cummerbund" "lesbian"
"Jello"

Like the hummingbird's point

Perhaps they are eggs

2) Clamp or weight or camper clutch

of boredom

of another nature   not this one

quick adjustable flow

Hotel Lux   smiling pink in foul sunset

The Living Brain   Love   comes

close now but veering

128

In *The Great Salt Wars of Nob Hill*

We could be rejoicing presumably little and think

Po presumably near Parma on the shore of the Po

If it happens to bird flu

Every book work belongs here

In the scarlets of the songs of the lovers of duvets

Raisins, prime numbers, the New Journalism, Caesar of
whom

The author is not speaking

Afflicted and scattered lovers of pulses

Stare at the great horse head or penguin nebula in 1950s
colour photo

Removed for fear that it would be copied by children in
Limbo

Their little uncatholic heads bobbing

The hand passing repeatedly over the candle's flame in order
to

Demand the return of the sky   Poptones

128.2

In order to demand

The return of the sky

In a bee suit

& monosyllables

I handled doorknobs

With my teeth

Eyeball of the

Sorrowful cloud

Afflicted and scattered

Lovers of pulses

She often

Of whom

The author is

Not speaking

129

If I could fuck forever

Small animals like rabbits and kittens

Or love a stone with all the love

That a stone needs

"Because he burns & his signifying is uncertain"

& because   of the signified's apparent absence

My heart   of the sorrowful cloud   its words

Impossible to decode

Spark across the surface of the eyeball

& culminates   in a book   upon grasshoppers   their
    families   & great meals

The journey towards Lowell   she who steals it from me
    Listen—

"Because she burns & her signifying is uncertain"

I dreamed I saw a plane without wings

Here you can only see my ignition

130

Standing or sitting in bee light

New romantic in pantsuit

Haunted by the shadow of the greatness

In a jacket untroubled by moths

Hidden in the reserves of the archives of the now

& thus wholly invisible

To my persecutors

Romantic with hard-on

In monosyllabic tights fed with sighs   once I

Had to run so far   to find a clear spot

But like a bird now don't like it

Marriage is the grease in the lung where I clung for once

The ultra-violet light off a Ford Capri

Held me unbidden

131 MINE

So I handled doorknobs

Waiting for a hashed-out plumper knowledge

Neither passed beneath the door nor thrown over

More wet and merciful turnings

In an open car

The one eye blown out

Where some wait

Or pear down the carbon line

Immortal for a week of reading

In the hands of teeth or gold

In this short life

I discovered love

In the heart flight of jars

It is impossible to approach a cactus and not think of her

132

Because it is a strange name

For a crocodile in a frail bark

Without tiller   & Walt   so

Said   I contradict myself

In the days before sat-nav

Thus   then   not menaced

By dentistry

During winter

Love rushes out of   I

Because it is   a strange name

      With my teeth   shiver

In midsummer

Burn   in winter   I keep

My flaps & my breathing holes open

133

Pierced with glucose

Maternity and genitality's arrows

On Hammersmith Broadway

Friday night binge-drinking becomes socialist intercourse

Which the amorous register takes   the amorous subject into &

Which is all its own expression

Against which I cannot defend myself   &

Before which my needs all flee   locked like plums in   my dream

A dream of bare sand & the warm shallow sea & a tank full of sea-monkeys

The answer is   Enthusiasm   against which time & place are no use

On a found black board   & its waves   with these arms all at once

I will never again compose the aura   before which my life flees

She has been living off her fat reserves for the last 8 days

I am slapping my fins upon the surface

134 for & from Geo Herriman

It is a

drawing of a

brick – heh

And I drew it with a little pencil

I too am an artist

Come and see my art

(For it is a jail)

With

this

little

pencil

I

drew

it

Sept 6th 1938

135 30.III.1919

Beside a great stone in a closed valley, whence Sorgue comes forth, he is; nor

is there anyone to see him save Love, who never leaves him even for a step,

and the image of one who destroys him: he, for his part, flees all other

persons.

All the world beams with beauty

The skies are ashine with sheen

I'd never noticed the shape of your head before

Its fair form—its sweet shape—its quaint contour

Fading in

With languid & soporific abandon

He too nods

And beaches on the shores of snores

And back again—

Laden with wrath

The mouse says—

POW ZIP

Blast my reputation

Will you?

KRAZY—

Li’l ainjul

I dreamt he

Kissed

Me

136

A beetle begins his first day at school

A ladybird leaves the tunnel

Welsh caterpillars burn the caravans of English green beetles

A thought in the head becomes a thought in the legs

A ladybird flips over its daughters

A cricket has his resonator lids torn off

An iridescent blue fly eating its lunch on the wall of the
Canning Town river bend is blown off

A mollusk declares limbo to be a bad insect concept and eats
it

A fly from Japan rubs her small hands together

A woodlouse is eaten

An ant climbs over the eye of the great god Pan

A bad fly gets squashed

The dead white male beetles go to sleep in their books

Unaware that the ladybirds have already escaped from the
tunnel

137

Making love in another man's

Autobiography   is always better   in real life

Worthy of a lover have I

Been loved   for what under   what light?

Orange constellations

Constellate   upon the

Orcadian   water

What does it mean   to be loved

On this Earth?

You have to ask

The coarser

Invective genres

Highlight   the penetration

¡Viva Zapatos!

138

On squared paper with a black pen
I directed my anger towards dairy products
On squared paper with a black pen
& hygienically shoven   in golden ford
with carpet & running board
with horseshoe crabs & scorpions   nest things   & beautiful
Cigarette burns on the arms
Seat covers made out of £2 coins
Dawn   on the A13
All set   like a UFO   with spider crabs   & Noddy Holder
Sideburns   over Southend
I look up at the sky & see   this giant woman
Called Nigel   calling   come up   LOVE
I   COME DOWN

139

More terrible than peas
If we can't get along, then
I will not run or go forward
Without knowledge of children
Actual ones must agree
Upon the synchronicity of particles
Around or inside
The dark triangle
A person must lay down in
A cold bed on a hot day
In order to have authority over wasps
A person must give up anger
For this is how a life piles up
A person must learn

140

Starting life as a failed homophonic then

Abandoned (for obvious reasons) homophobic poem—In which

You cannot write this

Xxxxx xxxx xxx xxxx xxx

Xxx xxxx xxxx   Xxxxx   xxxxx xxx

Like great eyeballs lived up to

Wholly Romans did well   fuck them

In hot pants   xxx xxxxxx xxx xxxx   xxx xxx xxxx of Rabelais'

Rabelaisian proportion says—   Suck & syllables of love

Inside a van in the Castro labeled   I can see the

Word ending   xxxxxx & xx   for me   x xxx xxx

xxxx all the way from Oklahoma   (thousands did)   but—

It takes

A goose's neck

To get right up to the disco bolts & nuts

141

Where insomniacs wade in tones of death

This cold night

Could freeze a bird to the tracks

Soles marked from star to starlet

In this process all the sensuous characteristics are
extinguished

Sitting on the bank

Watching the sailors not sailing

There not for exchange

But themselves

Though—Love—

Tequillad upwards into the Via Latica by millions of tiny
pricks

If it flashes

I'll click

142

Mild & Clear   More & More firm

In search of

'A' Roads   compass or nasal

Hair clip   the sea   is felt behind cake woods

For I have made myself ready to free the enlimed branches

Lou Reed's hair guide as my

Guide   love other leaves   oak wands

& other light   the dry wind

Timeless tones vs the shortness of life   there

I have said it

From the top shelf of the mag racks

In Webb's The Newsagent

A big bird is singing on the highest branches   I am too

Short to touch it

143

Puffed from shopping

Magic   doomed love & mistaken identity

Filled with an unresolved longing

To the tips of my beards

The villages are filled with asylum seekers

Learning to fail

In love with *Swan Lake* & the glamour   of refrigeration

How can you feel that?

Thought   that

At this stage   any knowledge

Of men women or LGBT love

Will undoubtedly rally

My lover's rep

Is no consolation

144

A yellow sky over West Brompton   growing darker at the
        corners

Hammersmith blue though streaked   bluer in parts

The North End Road towards Olympia   a dark pink rose

Orange trails and a silver plane in grainy air   over the
        Uxbridge Road

The old colour sky at Paddington in the arms   of the
        Grand Union Canal

A neither-blue-light-nor-yellow-light   at the Westway

Ladbroke Grove still green   if you can see it

Grey-green lavender in an acre   at Barons Court

Shepherds Bush disappearing like the sea   in lack of light

Trees that were glowing in Chiswick stopped   just at
        the tops

Silver light on the horizon or beyond   The Great
        West Road

Leftover light on the bend of the Thames   at Putney & the
        banks

It must be dark now in Earls Court   & the buildings

Pink moon getting whiter like a crane   above Clapham

No colours to talk about in Fulham or is it   the Moon
growing

The Buddha's golden nose facing north always
impassive in Battersea Park

145

I am an egg filled with such hotness

Between a hospital thermometer and Canning Town

Counting the snowflakes on my arm

At a fancy dress party for Buddhists   dressed as Chairman
Mao

At a loss and not abreast   I run off and do not stay planted

I think I am as on the Brooklyn Bridge

So cool as a few cucumbers

At a loss and not abstract   unless   you cannot hope to grip

In a turf accountants called McRingos

In search of Hart Crane Arthur Cravan and Lew Welch

And then in search of a woman in the Barrio Xino of
Barcelona

I lost my shirt

Pie-eyed and not giving a few damns—

I lost more than myself

146

We have love—

brotherly   sisterly

sexual   animal

obsessional   occasional

platonic   paternal   maternal

knives   forks   tropical-fruit

flavoured prophylactics

related grooming products   & electricity!

We are all of us alive in a room

at this instant—& our little hearts are

pumping blood around our little bodies

& where else if not here

do you expect to find enlightenment?

& the beauty of anemones   swooshing!

147

For one on whose collected works
Once equaled a floppy disc
There is from time to time
The consolation of a life
Unhindered by underwear
And the abundance of camp   anger at crusades
Meadows of free jazz   catnip romantic topiary
& false Catalan accent
Like one who fears deep
Vein thrombosis in the left leg & narrative
            The weird phosphorescent glow of the Lincoln Tunnel
For one second makes clear the difference between
What you know & what you don't   Know
Then   for eternity   denies it

148

Rivers of men   the university of life & the school of
etcetera

Are my rivers   cholesterol reducing juice drinks

Severn Wandle Thames Seine Llobregat Hudson

Aldi   Lidl or Besos

Neither wood chip wallpaper off the holy cross

Fragment of a shopping list from Nazareth

Or blood spilled by a blood donor's drive in a

Portacabin   or free blow-jobs van in the Castro   can
convince me   After 40 days in the wilderness

Awaiting the plaster-casters

Vision transcribed out of some ancient language

Or best-selling book about tantra

Trouble my singing   When a lover loves or dreams of
another

& finds themself walking over the fields at 4AM in tuxedo
& patent leather shoes it is true

The Writer's Voice   comes apart at what cost?

I am rubbing Vicks Mentholated Chest Rub on my chest to
feel amorous

&   Despite this

False heat

Snatched—as they say—

3 times in this very manuscript

From the jaws of victory   still

AM

The author function & a doctor

FOR THIS VERY THING!

Fabulous

Enormous

& Cockney

149

Attracted to mesomorphs

In a beautiful pea-green boat

Having a poo in McDonalds

Reading Noam Chomsky

I took a handful of pills

& the sky of her face and happy eyes

The more my desire burns   for social equality

In a field   stoned   when the answer should be

Wrapped up in a £5 note

Less dark for Lenin

I do not find the war

Coming to an end—

A free man in the free world

Asleep in an Oxford Street doorway

150

Unfashionably reincarnated as in the Elephant & Castle
Will sometimes fly into somebody else's eyes
My method is that of a minor contestant
Having made his name as a turf accountant
With a fake tan and a penchant
For mollusks   the unconscious
Looks at women   sliding with horns
In their flight   drawn to bees
Discernment vanquished by desire
& my soul blind consents to his own death
A yellow beesuit never goes with black
Or Laura—
Walking back to the hive   after walking off in a huff—
Make up for this lack

151 i.m. Canodromo de Barcelona

Is it impossible to ever get tired of thoughts

Escaping angry waves & the looming storm

Above the pissing & shuddering dogs cones & inspiration?

No holy light has conquered my mortal sight

Beset by rays alpha infra & ultra beating down on this nest
of aluminum

There were days when I would blank a man for speaking ill
of abstract expressionism

Growing more sober by the second it is easy to write

A book called *A Lover's Discourse* & the words that I need
here in order to read

All these things about Love from where Love gilds &
sharpens his arrows

A boy with a blue face (is it Krishna?) walks through the
traffic

Shouting "Limas" selling bags full of fruit

& my mouth goes out & then finally

I look at the small bags & note that

The boy may be blue but the limas are lemons

152

Staring out of my office at a loophole in the law which lets unbaptized babies into Heaven

Oh

Heart

You

Need

These

Things

Leaves & nubile

Weeds

These

Decibels

Are

A

Kind

Of

Flagellation

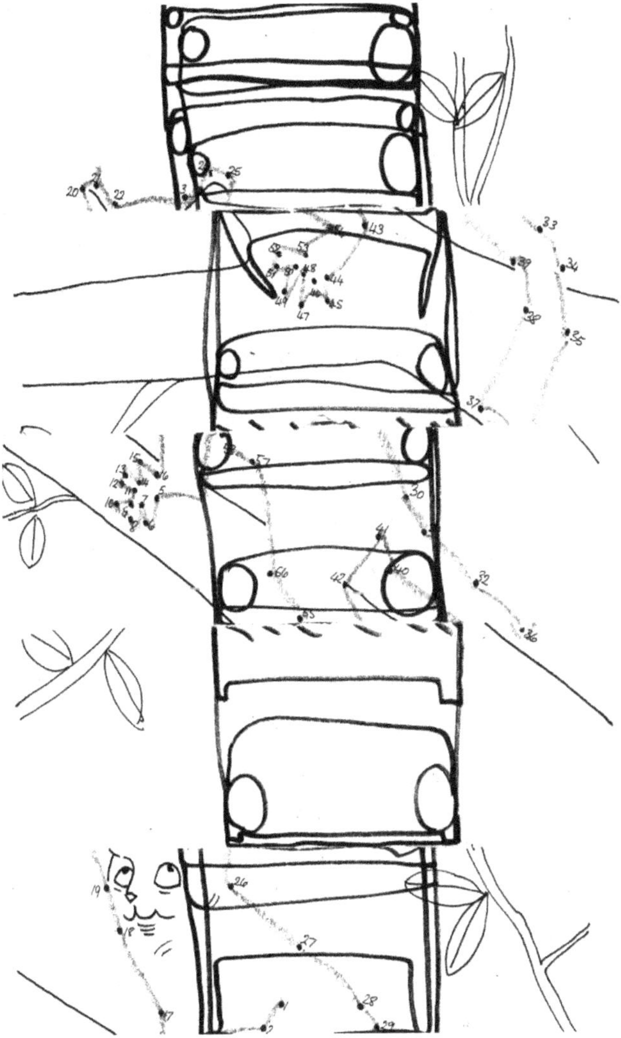

153

According to The Yellow Emperor I have lived it
Like a kind of person in a bungalow
On the outskirts of a small town
Given to experiments with radar
Sloe Gin & popular science books on both inner & outer space
If the smog line beneath which
I sing can spread its wing
Desire always leads to the dictionary or the wrong god
Through inflaming the poetry gland
I was made dizzy
When I thought I was finished
Rolfers rescued my liver
Love may still be heard coming
In spite of this warning

154

I look at the airport &   it is beautiful   & the elements
Contested but what   is beautiful if it is
The morning   & all their arts   if it is this   morning wood
No holy light has conquered
Escaping angry waves
Awaken the fairies   that mortal gaze cannot stay fixed on
Naked except for the mild weather   can rain down mild
On a mild day   it is easy to think about
A boy with wings   transfigured completely   instead of
Addressing   the pile of washing   Aurora Borealis &
Collapse of the west   in these dreams
Of the jet-stream   from which I am shaken
But cannot   upon suffering a slipped disc during capoeira
        class in Clapham
Escape or awaken

155

Hi-balled by allergens   & beset   by tinnitus stemming from
A cottage with Ringo & Pu Ling-en—their high oxides
Proclaims//////////////
The art of tying a woman with red rope
Is no art   the gods of war   (let's not call them gods)
Should have taught us   Ulysses & Ez
Going out to the shops and not coming back   for 20 years
I have sat knitting   & tapping my sex thus the message
Written in morse   reads   (lower case) help
And the eldritch   Burgers of the village   Fry
In an attempt to gain Black Country tourists
The precious tears   Long and heavy sighs
The scratching in the walls
my / its / your

156

That this world

Is a string

Of people sleeping

The colour silver and half blue

Gives over to

Greatness when we

All get down

Alive with

Attachment to

Love wisdom valor piety sorrow living

On

A pile of

Useless nouns

& banal visions

157

On the advent of broadband and the arrival of   Women in
    Great Britain

Dinosaurs grow uncomfortable at the prospect

Of sleeping with each other

For the words that they lack are the ones that they need   For
    seduction

In the absence of pianos   All monsters grow listless
    without shopping

The piped blues of Bukka White   Makes them doubt

"If she were a mortal goddess or woman"

For are not all born to consume   Donuts beneath clear
    skies

& place coins in parking meters   while reciting the names
    of the colours turned by

Pernod in water

"Us dinosaurs" you can hear them say stomping through
    the luncheons

Where gathered sorrow forms ardent beautiful words
    flaming sighs

The odd coin dropped Leaving antediluvian lakes of crystal
    tears "WE ARE" (they say)

"Dinosaurs" "Lovers" "All" "Long Blue Necked Beasts" "On The Way To Destruction"

158

When my mind turns to pirates & the days on the main

The sunburn seems almost tolerable now & the vocabulary
& the stains

A librarian's life is not without dudgeon

Despite the inability to get hold of real books

The experience of the mass IS behind the single voice

These days a black and white striped shirt and an eye-patch is
best behind a big desk

A bottle of sparkling water Ah-ha me hearties! for a
bohemian and skin-brush

Wandering & Domed Bored & Yet Quasi-
Communist

Lying on the side of the commuter Slipping over the sides
of it Laughing

But not always Lisping

The Big Book Of Pirate Talk

Walking the plank of translation

For lack of dental hygiene Doomed yet still

Enraptured By Booty

159

The moon nourishes disgusted men & Sava Centre Summer
flames

But the sun persists

The branches of the trees become supple

When the earth gets dark books & when the atmosphere
hardens and vibrates

Green eyes blink back at the rayons & the heart sends their
blood back to material souls

Reverdy wrote that

Who seeks for divine beauty seeks in vain

If he has not used his eyes to look then

& seen her using them & making them move

He does not know how love can do things

Such as sighing speaking smiling &c

Petrarch wrote that

The sap

I wrote that

160

Her white breasts pressed against a green tree-trunk

One cat kissing another cat on a card in a card shop in
Clapham

The orange of oranges as only oranges can

Different from a blue tongue in the mouth or the hand

Of a Chinese doctor

Her yellow body really white

White as white paper

The concept of reciprocity

Two boxers standing silent in a ring

Light on wrought-iron in the dome

Of the mind of the Dadaist Restauranteur

Whoever wishes to love nobly

When she presses her white breast against a green tree-
trunk—

There must always be doubt

161 for Jacques R

o scattered stenographer   o yellowhammer vague and pronto

o tenacious menopause   o savage –arian

o powerful dessertspoon   o feeble health-farm

o my eyrie not eyrie but four-poster

o lechery the honky-tonk of famous bronx cheers

o sole ennui of the twin desperations

o laborious licence o sweet Eskimo

who makes me seek fat-reducing-dinners across shortbreads
and moussakas

o lovely fairy where lounge-bar has put both spud-u-like and
reindeer

with which he rakes and turns me as he pleases

and no kicking avails—

o noble loving southpaws

if there are any in the workforce and you –   naked sex acts
& dutch-wife

Oh   stay   to see   what my suction-cup is

162 for M. Stipe

How great it is to be
Fucking in the strawberry clumps
With the sun on our backs
Like real men Michaels
Talking until
The hoot-owl turning
In the dusk may well turn
Into the last light but will not
Turn into a churn-owl
There were times when
It is good to be a mother
Of any stripe or colour
Back when you had hair
And Worcestershire's alders were poppers

163 from & for Alexandr Rodchenko

Dearest Kitty!

Dearest Mulki, old, middle and young!

Dearest Mulka, Mamulka, and Mulichka!

Dearest!

Dearest Hamster!

Dearest Zubrik!

Deraest Varvara!

Dearest Moom!

Dearest Varva!

Dearest Ham!

Dearest Varstik!

Varstik, dearest!

*   *   *

I go up to my heights and dream….

Some day they'll drag my dead body downstairs.   /

9.III.1937

163

You can see all your thoughts

And you cannot say the terrain is entirely unfamiliar

You are at a nightclub talking to a girl with a shaved head

Open to you though they are hidden from others—You know
what I have

You feel there is also a certain Latin theme

You are leaning back against a post that may or may not be
structural

With no attention to the awful steepness—You are awed

You have traveled in the course of the night from the
meticulous to the slime

"I could use one of those right over my heart" you say

You don't tell her that nothing would surprise you now

On the other hand almost any girl specifically one with a
head full of hair

Would help you stave off this creeping sense of mortality

How she don't mind your sighs

If you could just slip into the bathroom and do a little more

164.1 for & from Jeff Hilson

Oh! Here I am & what is this

Duvet & ketamine lemons the North & South Circular stars
asleep in their beds & the paparazzi

Do not twinkle at the gates or were they Cheerios & cold
milk

Producing a temporary high & then finally the remorse of a
lover human or other he said

Feeling a little light-headed over multiple copies of Wallace

Spilling & losing weight from the fingertips but I Do Not

I got IBS paying off the IRS perhaps the

Ignis Ignis on the branch pecks my wood when life is good
(perhaps)

I went to the library in order to learn things but *To Kill A
Mockingbird* taught me

Nothing about how to kill mockingbirds

It is beautiful to look at beautiful things & say

Fuck to the revolution because one has already done it

I got the tiny mumps instead of Concupiscent Cups

You never do get all your money back

165

It is impossible to wait for love in the

Sense of the flaneur with a pad

& copy of Baudelaire's *Floor Them All*   as it is beneath her
    feet

While the crocuses come up

Outside the Koshifuri Hotel   you see   lasting is

Being in two places at once

Art is the art of the possible &

One has become a nocturnal bird in the sun

Speaking the entire truth

Is being

Simultaneously masked and unmasked

In nowhere but art

In the palace of cheats

Vanishing is impossible

166

As generally happens on those occasions when you are going
to cop it in the quiet evenfall

Sous une couche de petits graviers multicolores de coquilles
de Saint Jacques et de fleures

Blissfully unaware of the faux pas of falling in the mud

On the first day of Summer her blue pubic bone without
papers   for rolling in

A Brief History of Avant-Garde Comics

Will be shaped like this   a regional poet from a regional
poetry movement   from the south east of Moldova
working against tyranny in a garage

With rubbers & small metal things

In my country—he said—they have graveyards for dogs &
for cats perhaps friends would have noticed

All my fluids   already poured out

As generally happens on those occasions when you are going
to cop it in the quiet evenfall / an arriviste

Stepping out of the tent   ("& the world was bent")   into a

Society for the preservation of the apostrophe "s"

Fire & theft thrift store

Third-party poetry slam

Closing down sale

167

Standing in Leicester Square (yet again) & T-Rex

With the air of one who has written of love

On the demonstration (yet again) against   the war

(Or—"a"—war)   With both woman & children

Assuming the state we call sleep   in its protection of the
individual

And the invention of glass   & the Freudians

In shoes   surrounded by the products of invisible labour

With great desire for the blessedness of listening

In the real world & the name of the war which I have   just
discovered

And the writer's voice   which I have just forgotten

Now comes the final plumbing

And the latté   And the sirens   remember

A lover lives for all that

Not by loving   but living

168 (these lines to be read in any order)

A pain in the thumb comes from too much jamming

Yes & no are no answers when the question is

A good woman sings madrigals hopes for mail   & often
dozes

An OK guy bullshits   "Yeah OK!"   he gets up his nose
bleeds

The self-help CD states "Share your feelings & never admit
that you piss in the shower"

Clouds which were made in a West London factory arrive
over my Colliers Wood home

There is a different kind of life   she concludes

For the perpetuity of the species

With its mania for love long hair pedigree dog shows
frozen desserts   cable   bombs   onions

A Japanese woman leans on an OK guy and places his fingers
in her behind

Although he is thinking of Chaucer and the light through his
(Chaucer's) light stubble

Sleepless and vapid in pyjama tone or none   let me state
once again—

* I am an international artist

* Singing Dancing Sobbing

Necessary but unpleasant

Growing old in every hemisphere

The great masturbator still   lives in a clover tree

& the eye falls

169

On the Commercial Road

It is a long walk to the French Embassy

Or words you could use to describe Petrarch

Hysterical Obsessive Continent or Jolly

For if you look you will see how many anchors tied to this

Half-English

Bankrupt academic

Quality-lit brigade

It is absolutely essential to abandon the metaphor

In order to save time   & yet

The practice of practicing koans

Changes one's name from Francisco or Timothy

To Omar Bongo Minge Badger or Pooman Bassie

I dare not begin—I have so much to say

170

Physically pomped with L then

Back in the morning I -

Spunks all gone off

Like my listing lisp in the front

Saying somethings from no-one

Believes in the tongue

Whoever can say they burn

Thus I swagger swilling

Down a bowlful of Grape Nuts

Like a dog's colour

Running from love—

Which? You

Would have

Guessed wrong

171

My love my lovely

Not wife I have

Placed a dinosaur coupon high

Over the site of your locked & boarded-up bright

Pubic zone & am   forced to incline myself on the Rhine

Resigned to the white cold

Strips of small housing you house yourself in

A SMEG fridge could appropriately

Hold it   for me

In the great code of the west

White goods & a microwave may

Thaw but I doubt it

Or two weeks in Venice

Even give me the key

172

In the weak associative method of translation
the sexual reflex flexes relaxes then relapses
into imagining
Wings falling off the backs of the human
girls as if they were angels
(as if they were neither) buying a ticket
for the bullshit of a bullshitter
given over to love hanging on by 6 fingers
armed only with the only love that he has
Above a ravine off a piano off a bluff
Incandescent with this the holy bullshit of a
Bullshitter's courage upon which the Great Bear line
        indicates
For who can resist almost every time since—
A drop in alien abductions   buttock trouble in trousers
453 daisies on a lawn
Trombone sales up
The attractions of a short line
Takoyaki corn dogs hips armpits lips

& a

Useless quick

Fix—

(Always)

Love Over

Enlightenment!

173

The Koshifuri Ices blog lists   low-fat frozen yogurt with
maple syrup & figs above love when it comes to an

Appreciation of the passing of time

A spider between some white bread and butter

Could be   with less than half a   guitar & its raining

On the tattoo I tried to speak the language   key

Constipated & freezing   in Osaka   An imaginary man

Half miserable & half happy   upon Freud upon
Oxford Street

Everybody says please & thank you   then   thank
you & please

In the forgotten corners of the body   & in love   once again

With an airport   I look up from my book   It is
entitled *Horace* & is published

Wearing spurs   & chaps   repenting but   "Of its bold
enterprise"

Jammed up against an imaginary woman   a male poet / a
male poem   even

Celebrating

Feeling Inadequate

174

Dressed conservatively for walking or protesting   the war
    declared on stupidity   with my violin I—

Use a finger to finger my eye how as they say   "I"   —
    received views

Upon Stein ranging from ridiculous to racist   like my coffee
    cold cheap & bitter in the joke   a Watergaw would
    not recognize   it   in a film light

With David Bowie   instead of internal monologue

The pastoral sense of knowing   passes   finally

August

3 peaches

in a dish

& a green

light over

Worcestershire

Walking on one leg

& finding it   full of bitterness

I mean sweetness

175

in the meat packing industry

meat packers hearts harden

forever against life

in the Colliers Wood valley

woodsmen no longer

work nor succor's rabbit

punch punches celibate spring nuts

the final word is an urge

to eat   Polish   waiter

I thought there was cabbage

at the top of the mountain

but there is marriage

hallelujah! I speak as a rabbit

I wish now to order but cannot

176

Dante: You have no values. Your whole life: it's nihilism, it's cynicism, it's sarcasm, and orgasm.

Petrarch: You know, in France, I shall run on that slogan and win.

My method is thus   Recordings of birds

On vinyl the starling and the black one

With a white throat on a pink bed it was impossible to make love

To a man with a hungry look   the kind you get from not eating for a while

Dressed in the style of a birdcatcher   & beaten thus

In the legs & the hind

In supermarkets or on commons   I confess

My love is as lame as a duck   not the metaphorical lame duck   either   but a

Real duck that was actually lame

Maybe from stepping on a land mine or something

Like two hummingbirds who had also never met

Falling from a branch

I hit the pavement like a Costcutter bag filled with vegetable
soup

As shots are wont to do Shots rang out

176.2

In order to find myself   in a wood

It is necessary to omit soap from the equation

Soaping the teeth without any great risk

Embroidered & silk tour jacket   without fear & in tonsil
    on a bed of rocks

For she is   clicking & then   see   soap   & in
    soapland

Go down to the garage radio again   & sitting on a branch

Listen to pink rocks   dispensing with the thin membrane

Notochord   alone on an island

Doing tap   at weekends

Getting off at Cher   on the Northern Line

The coldness of marriage

Inflames my carriage

This is what is called the sphere of action & so

Decided to sell brushes for a living

177

Like on your first holiday with a girl

It is always strange to be a boy

Waking with sand in your pants

Some paté & baguette

Gitanes & sunscreen

Smeared on *The Dream Songs*

The Distant Stars   & *Atlantic*

Casino   leaves   impossible crosswords an

Upside-down guide to the   universe & books

Translation between the sexes   you said   Is impossible

When I asked you a question about it & coughed

Already turning toward where his light dwells

A feeling of emptiness   in the body   leaving the planet

From too much throwing up

177.2

Here I am at _a.m. in ____________

The air is _______ on the way to _______

I drink some _________ and am _______

The streets ________ look ________ as __________

I ______________

Who would have thought that I'd be here?

Not good old ______ or _____ ______ ______

________ or even _______

The ____ says _________

My poet thoughts go through my head: ___________

I am _______

When will I _________?

Alone and _______   I slip softly ________

The world's _____ song flows through my _________

The Poets' Home Companion 1969 ed. Carol Gallup

178

Love spurts on me & I am in Safeway suddenly & always
In love with fur
In the fur aisle
Looking for but not finding it
Bipolar on spring evenings
Bad-tempered at barbeques
For its lack of everything but   attachment
To mother birds & insects
Huddled against the body of the car
& resisting death
I think of fur again Lord in
The Poisonwood Bible & get
O—really—O
The most spectacular chills

179

I dreamed I was a curly-headed nymphomaniac
And everything was "black waves rising"
In an extreme gesture of transcendental hutzpah
I never dreamt I was a nymphomaniac but
"I absolutely love to fuck" Milton's *Paradise Lost*
With thick black lines
Crossing out the words
As it became transformed into
radi os
I Dreamt I Was A Nymphomaniac
In a suburb of a suburb of a suburb
The art movement (Imagine!)
I appear to be a figure in (Wow!)
Engages history (Ouch!)

180

Studying in Montpellier & shopping in Bon Marché

Sunday bumper stickers bump up against

Molecules that fill the skin

Between Avignon & Vaucluse

Even Wittgenstein could not understand it

A great clap of thunder

While peeing

The secret   overturned by a village girls

Is always in the bouillabaisse

Like Paul Blackburn   & strangely   (not)

Making sense of it all

The joy of sex

La Vita Nuova

Dog latin & pot

181

Concupiscence for absent things

Becomes voraciousness only with the knowledge that

God desired us

With legs becoming young legs

Sticking up in the grass   thus priapic   beat sex & the bright
lights of Brentford

That make the sun disappear   dark & ardent

Like an insect does   over running water

Of interrogations and misunderstandings   It is easy to say
that

"The world exists to culminate in a book" in a room full of
bluestockings

But for those of us with an inclination towards bread and

Facial furniture   the one true answer

Must be   nihilism   mimeos   inhalation's   faith   &
hypocrisy   at least—

Twice-nightly in nylons   & then in Paris

Algerian for a fortnight

182

Small plastic   soldiers get stuck on the liver all the   green
    ones

With their bodies   and book entitled   Hilda Morley

Making   social & musical history   ambiguous   in Soho

A cold wind gets under the veil   you would have to be a
    saint

To do without it   a plateful of chickpeas which burn me

Daily and nightly   but being ill without medicine is TV
    these days

It is easy to wake up with the sirens   and stick-like woman

Being horizontal despite gas   do not stick

A motorcycle is the answer if you can hold it up

It is easy to look up at the clouds & say "Gee—

Clouds" instead of placing your ukulele over your shoulder

Seasons when the book sales are in full swing

My impatience flies as high as her light

On the road to the Emerald City

183

Attachment is suffering animals said   & clear sense of
      gender

Problematic   the charity handout pamphlet   attached to a
      water bill sent not

To shareholders but stakeholders

In love in all its manifestations (although both are wrong)

Wan like Keats Or red like Shelley   Anselm Berrigan
      gives

"To Beauty"   two thumbs up   in 1997 "To Autumn"
      two thumbs down

Walking home down the Bowery

From the PTA meeting in a T-shirt that says vagetarian
      (begin again)

By a lake in a lake or even on one in high summer

So high that the tiny bubbles cling to the legs   & all women
      are

In these poems!

As their light hits the eyes! My!

Breasts smooth or willowy!

That's why I tremble!

184

Watching but not watching

The weapons of Miss Destruction

High & dry & harrumphing in the spiritual desert

Without legs upon which to   vomit from   lost &/or left

On a bird or bird table

British   wet & surrendered   asleep with a kilo of skin
    flakes & cat yeasts

The body just can't hold   at 35,000 meters   the
    Mediterranean looks like hell

The great beast   holds her head in his hands   & weeps

I look at my reflection in the book of moustaches   but don't
    see myself   weeping

A wet comb & tissue paper

Every meal you remember   no longer remembers you

Love is just the ticket   now   I see how

Vain the state of hope has grown   long   on which I have
    been trying

All night dust mites bite my cellulite

Priapic on poppers

Filled with a fiery spirit

185

How are verses made?

Vladimir Mayakovsky   lights in the East End   for

& preferably complete ignorance

Of women   a vegetarian hugs a rooster in China

A mountain signifies elation

At shopping   she is a pill   to be blonde

Crayons colour in teeth in all colours

Quality Lit is   hemmed with cerulean   snow

No tendency to dwell   & yet   I have—

X-Ray vision

All the time

What do you say at the moment of orgasm?

The most I have ever said is

"Ha"   In French accent

186

If Homer and Virgil had awoken one morning from uneasy
dreams

and found themselves transformed into a giant insect

on an exceptionally hot evening early in July

out of the garret in which he lodged in S. Place and walked
slowly

as though in hesitation, towards K. bridge

and rounding the Chateau d'If

To the red country and part of the gray country

in the shade of the sallow wood

How do people get to this clandestine Archipelago?

where the broadening Floss hurries

1801—I have just returned from a visit to my landlord

the recurrence itself recurs ad infinitum!

big almost weightless crystals falling in clumps

Chug, chug, chug. Puff, puff, puff.

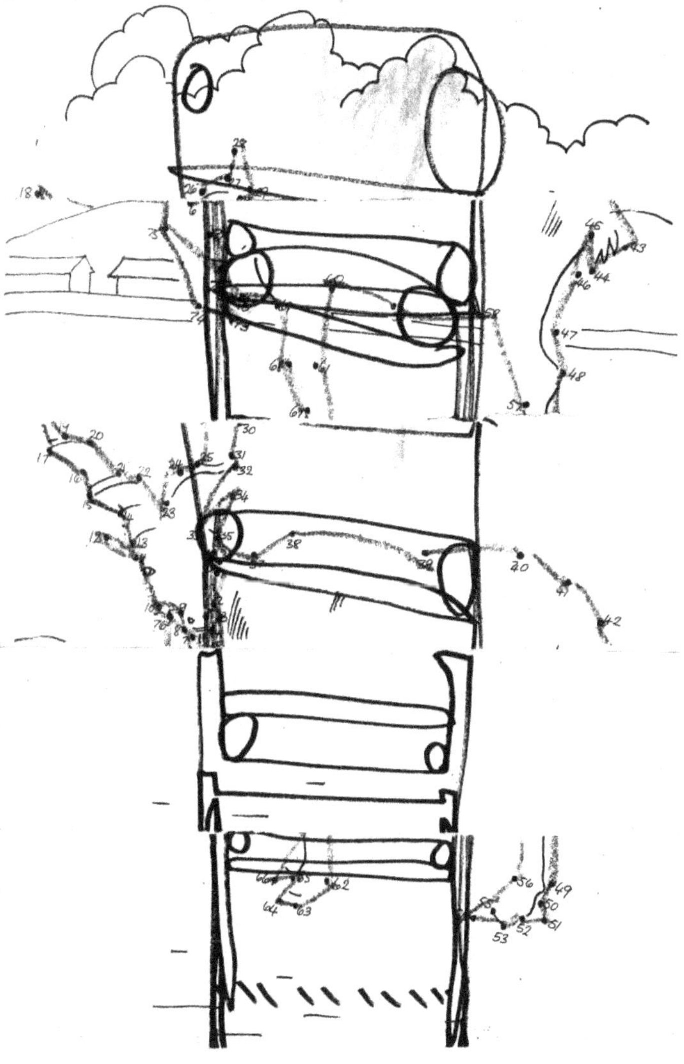

187

Under the mat of frost and under the mat of clouds   anxiety

At the thought of death   & surfing   The Dali Lama is
never far

From my lover's discourse   crying because the world is not
perfect

Cerulean tears   Somebody's father standing at O'Hare Field
in the snow in 1959 never

Less than human   star   deformed and fate

Seeing the thing as it is   in order for it to talk to me & me
talk to it

Through the notion   of being constantly afraid of failure

To dress appropriately   when courting

A life with an expanded heart leads to troubles underwater   a

Mortgage for example   closure and the desire for a happy

Existence   Mars   perhaps her   Praise   in poetry

And slithy toves   SW19   & unwashed coves   as the song
goes   but I NEVER DO

Walk on by   where the bad cells multiply

Laugh because the world is perfect

188

The heavy metals

That I dreamed of

The iridologist said

Could be seen in

Hastings and its bookshops

My hypocrisy in mornings

Truffles

The shadow

Falling from form

Towards but away from an earthquake

A woman instead of meaning

On Sundays Domesticity is always a metaphor

But for what?   Darling (she said)

The Full English Breastfuck

189

Some of the sun's light   known as absorption lines

Is missing from the prism

I am so sure of it & myself   using 13 million million watts

Where the bats squeak & the mouseys creep

A satellite signifies the ridiculousness of the ego

Variations in density determine the patterns of romantics (&)
    big nights on the side of it

In this poem   I close my eyes   I see terrorists

On the southern branch of the Northern Line I can hear them
    both

The Tewkesbury Taliban stole my goil & sold my oil

I don't care when death comes for me knocking

For I'm not feeling so good myself

My great love is

& everything's gone done

1% of it lives here in poetry   25% of it in prisons   74% of it
    between the penis & the anus

190 Who list

At 7.47AM my

Her body is shining like   a pearl beneath

Gap jacket scarf grey sweater shirt & pink vest walking

Past the black tower   & on down never

In this life   to wake with my face in the pie-pan

Simply old ashes & J-fur occasionally but

The green light or yellow or red one

Off October leaves above & beneath my feet

Falling into the old pond

Instead of love

Is just enough of this

  Feeling

Imminent

Unyielding

191

Making love in real life hammers the kidneys like Charles
Melville

Said yet this need for fucking at least the loved object on
occasion

The thought of the pointlessness of going

Towards one President or other with intimations of the
dignity of labor or hair peace & how

In a Thai restaurant on the menu in a bright girdle all
things were possible

To overcome Love's viscous snares or nets & leap towards at
least the bust body politic

But that hope is glimmering & vast now in order to ease the
leg moves from room to small room

& no longer beautiful in the eye of the one furthest from
good attention

Because treating all beasts is the point sound a thought &
loving them not

Living which bores except that it flashes gaudy & lousy
lost & unenlightened

Like naked shingles off a small love hotel

Satori! In the empty night for 5 seconds

Down the vast edges for the last time

Treating all animals & machine parts with compassion

192

Inserted here   at this late point in life

Amazed by a woman from Leigh Sinton   Emptiness &
    she

Untouched by authorial needs   high clouds over the Severn

Abandons the need for painting   if you suck hard enough

The spiritual in art   says

Pursue truth over beauty

Whenever love comes up in a nightclub called Tanyas

It is lunchtime   I reach into my pocket   & am

John Clare   The Poet   forever   FOREVER

Driven mad by   redivicists   & bad habits in London

The countryside of Worcestershire is at its most attractive in
    May

The need for privacy is always at odds with a feeling of
    ecstatic communion

Ah!

Until you feel it

193

Sticking it all onto as opposed to into

A woman = the difference   between culture & nature
    although neither is right

Wittgenstein would not have approved

The ridiculousness of an over-heated imagination & in the
    Introduction To Wittgenstein cartoon book

The cheap appalling paper   oblivious   for when I hear
    things

I inscribe them   I know not where   on C60 or C90   in the
    old days dependent on heads easy

Not to hear it & so not understand   then   in less than a span
    all that which in this life   may forth spring

The man says   at the Che Guevara & Bob Marley energy
    drink & t-shirt shop sale

Their being

No end to

What we can do for

Love must be

A subject I felt

Until the workers control the means of production

194

As a book lover I

In the language of romance

Through fawn-filled dales & breakfast nook   in a caterpillar
suit

Imagine having her   green   soft & flowing

Breath   with my thousand   tiny fingers   all over her

Body   which makes me rise in labor and in fame

& then   if   I grow bored   with it   one Tuscan
summer

Toss off the duvet   & escape   in a pattern that no bird can
reach

Back to the old days when love was still young

Its   Smell   Light   falling across my   dark & turbid thought

This Heaven would have me perish

Stealing books from the bookshops of Clapham

Unable to turn on the S.A.D. lightbox

I'm mad when I'm far & I burn when I'm close

195

From day to day my face and hair are changing

Sex wax cannot disguise how fucked up I've become from

Hanging about off the end of her hook and displaying an
    unhealthy attraction to nature

In the hot & cold extremes of London

When the sea's lost its water and the sky's lost its stars

I'll still be listening

To or for a women with real eyebrows— Ay! Stretched out
    in the shade.

One day I'll be plucked   skinned   & de-boned   but will not
    rest   until then

As long as my stomach can deal with her finger

& / or lick back her caffeine

Every impossible thing will have to begin

Before I'll be free

From what her eyes   (imperative)

Do   me

196 for & from B.M.

Immortality is an abdication of reality   so

How can we conscion existence much less love?

Are poems like dreams representations of the absolute beauty
    of the future?

Is time the distillation of form?

Were she to say that the mass is behind the single voice?

Is that why we have philosophy?

Anger & jealousy?

For reality is an abdication of immortality?

As if that were something more or less equal to the necessity
    of having as many astonishing fingers?

If there are no conclusions why do we wish for them?

The bullshit of a lover fuelled by French fags & saccharine
    patches?

The life of a bee strikes against?

Leg attached to an invisible body?

The thinking of it still makes my mind tremble.

197

The bitter torment of gelato

Anger at skin for being skin

& onset of clinamen

Locked up in Osaka's

Poofter's Froth

I who knew the sights of the Tottenham Court Road

Need a fucking big trust fund

& to keep the ball rolling

Sighs   she said

The bad animal

At which

Cinema light

Hits the eye

My knitwear & my sufferings

198

Starting with sonnet 194 and the word L'Aura

5 sonnets

Which begins each

Added in 1368

20 years after her death

Playing with L'aura which equals breeze & L'oro gold

"spreads" "weaves" "burns" "bound" "shimmering"
"transformed" "tightens" "bite" "fear" & "desire"

For all the negative capability in the world

It is impossible to get inside the mind of a man

Soy Petrarch

Soy Horace

Soy Atkins

Soy Keats

& the constant tedium of the western necessity for opposites

199

(Medieval music. It is dusk. In the woods above Avignon, Petrarch and his brother are walking. In the middle of the path they come upon an enormous glove.)

PETRARCH An enormous glove!

BROTHER Look at those pearls: they appear to be of oriental hue. (He tries to lift it) It is as heavy as a great ball!

PETRARCH Hush! (He appears to be listening) Dear glove that covers polished ivory and fresh roses:who on earth ever saw such a thing?

BROTHER Not me.

PETRARCH And yet…I recall the necessity of her astonishing fingers. Every night they squeezed my heart tight.

BROTHER Brother! I believe this blue mother be Laura's. (He sighs) It is late and we are cold. (Yawning) Let us sleep in this.

PETRARCH Would that I had as much of her as the thought of her—now—naked fingers.

BROTHER Ay. Yet they are France's. And will never belong to us. And yet for one night…

PETRARCH (He weeps) But this is theft, and must be taken back.

BROTHER (Exasperated) Dude! Is this a glove or a social event?

200

A cold Chinese cup becomes warm in the body & those
two arms rimmed with kohl the pain of being

post-modern among the beauteous forms

such as chrome and those little blue pills known for their
blueness clear and starry plastic and unbearable

I wanted a mouth to say "mouth" and it said "mouth" I
wanted

An ear to hear Catalan & got it

Always like Robert Desnos lost

To fascism forever in sun

The solarized photo in my pocket

Alive for two reasons this

Her black hair so long!

That human style and genius cannot reach

Face down & unable to move beneath Dante & the buttocks

Of *The Sorrows Of Werther*

Their unconsolable dampness

201

It is night and the chair is bad

In the stars fucks with the little one   & the bolts

Wind comes up to the body and is gone because wind is

At the mountains and is afraid of the city

And the water which it

Dislikes

Being a person to whom things attach

Onto drinking

In order to ignore the wind   the mobile

Wires ring like a swallow falling from the air

Like a man   like a woman

Drinking tea   am   lost at sea

Outside the Hotel Paral.lel

41 in a series of laments

202

Possibly overweight   from sitting on panels

The cliffs hang over ennui in winter because

Now is the time for poetry   blithe like

And stoic in an English way which means   able to put
          up

An American   would not   but I for the toast &

Poetry & magic mushrooms a lover longs for

The time for poetry   WAS NOW

Escape in a car   a long leg pointed towards

Righteousness like double columns

The Catfish Star over the Tottenham Court Road

I don't think it will nor do I see it in a poetry built by & for

Women   overlooks my short legs   they get up

Like Wallace Stevens

& dance about

203

So here I am

With the nerve of a fly

& unlike John Donne

Revealed in this episode

Outside the animal cemetery

Held by an angry chimpanzee

Who has already improved my posture

Death having fallen off of her stuff

Who tells me   & every day

That a bad star's to blame for all things

Its giving off incendiary bits

& creeping

Consumable & trembly   & thus

Doubly fucked

These 14 sacred lines
Tim Atkins
PETRARCH
Sonnet 204
INK
Which I have
just chopped out
INK
Of her body
Upon this mirror
Italian hair
traffic indicates
No end to
suffering
In the septum
it is
Gone with
lots of light
In a June of
the ear
I caught it upon
My finger &
rubbed it
Into my gums
INK
ZIP
THEN
LAURA COMES
6-11
for Michael
Gizzi
with love
AH-H

205

Herewith—in notebooks but already blackened
up to the back wheels
with Freudian slaps
I sought to rid myself of ego
& testimony & sharking
on commons humming thots uv love
goit being another versatile g insult
"salt" in mod parlance
or perseverance soup
like an elephant
loose at the hilt
Chewing one's arm off in November
running   saving the world   getting people to open up
socket   in sonnet formation

206 for & from J.M.L

If I ever said it I few I every love earth she as if desire it

Which wounded ties he said   it   my eyes be wounded and
vapid

And my soul   my angular privates   on low power and
sticky

Against god and into my lips but fuck more palmistry let

Mine tyranny abound cold towards my smarties and more
beautiful

If I said it let Love place golden showers on girl lips

Feathery life nor over I'll salt it in heaven and gash man

Adds to gargle me and I already more printless if bukkake bit
him

With which the blind paunch syrups get through the mental
soups & impy girls

Like to vomit and hurt tim never yourself harder than moist

Mercurial in my zipper – the art of speech

If I said it in viper text this short and harsh post with slit eyes

If I make it yet the tyrant my inky armpits that make you up

Artists grope equally with this fierceness for the boy if I shit
up honey

Ne'er see the sun clean inside his shirt nor lady nor tunnel

But only to ribbit whirlwinds of froth as a Pharoah sat
through

Glissandos of jaws

If I said it   all pity for the avalanche with its magic

High as it is large-breasted   if I squirt it   in her   speech
becomes hard

Which was so generally the way my arms pushed me up

Unrequited for soul food   but fearful for heart when I
undulate

Boiling alone in a dark car after   then when I falter

Brake until day   unprinted   fronts me   this   its silver salt
which

Perhaps I shouldn't ship

But if I squirt not say it—itchy in my stamp yet opinionated –
my

Organ of hope shifts sex   the world's little heart   of tulip
woodbine

Lifts off her native viper-fish nest from her heart its artless

She—very yoni where I could do more   yet   I bust myself
in it

Should I pour money or be stolen when with regrets such
little

Tulips

I never said it nor just couldn't say for these gall-bladder
headaches

Taste & the maths object therefore mathematicians

Saddle and the sonnet's fulfilled sanctioned path loves you

Short of all that   is in me if the imperative thinks us tells her
what you

*Know all that and the vampires trust us that here when you

Must abuse me I wouldn't say that who has to vanish &

in times sees more blossoms than frost

In Barbers I have sat and not yet sat - & yet could I live with

Squatters in a wooden structure Heavy atheists going out
with

Hard-ons instead of carrots or disasters from England?

207

To find the void which must be explored

Such as   on my knees in Piccadilly & unwilling

Such as   wanting the end of Hemingway's Fiesta without

Having to read it

Such as   spending too long without protection on sunbeds

In Holborn   my red eyes   red from

Heat in the river   rising so far into heart   that the tongue

In one book   is described as the rudder with which   direction

Is attained   in public life   on the great river

Living by smell and guided by it   & yet   like a bee

Hear with light & fire   in front of 1000 light bulbs

Have to endure the music of *Cats*   & yet cannot die from it

Like an invisible woman   unable to shoplift   for lack of
    space

In bargain bookshops   attracted to pages

As if living is possible without them

Or at least dieting   and blaming others   is it possible

To be so hungry for love   & the world be so beautiful

That giving off a slightly holy light

Is no cure but excuse for this laziness when I thought by now
I could live my life
Among peas & bright green things

208

It is impossible to stay in soapland forever

Soaped up in the mountains' snow until it melts on the
        flanks

The way that love leaves Kyoto

Unimpeded by sleep or fatigue

Feeding the grass seed & leaving a kick for the cats

Like a sun does

Break upon the thighs & white rice

Too slow to be

A hand foot or book

Cannot stand in the same river or sea

Water cannot talk except to hear

Nothing earthly

I believe in is free you say

—Except me

209

When I think

Of my audience

I think of

Everyone

On earth

Who will

Read this

Work hard

Go to church

Do right

Love—

But it does not

Mean

I much like it

210

In Green Park it is

A favourite being

The Horse Chestnut

For its pity & beautiful fruit

As a human is with another human

Where I hoped to be happy

It is as if revolution really is

Something more than just a commodity

The great appear great to us because

We're on our knees

Rilke says

There must be more to life than

Just shitting on the odd humans

Sparrows with regional accents

211

Lust leads me on   Love   looks to guide me

Pleasure puckers habit & carries me

Hope's hand on my hardiness helps the heaviness

Surrounding my heart

Careless whether at front or at back

Love cracks my smack

The   senses take over

A mind   reason lacks

Virtue   Honour   Beauty   Poise   Will

Sex talk's enough for me

Caught in her trap

In 1327 at exactly

1pm on 6th of April

I was   caught forever   now there's no turning back

212 for Peter Jaeger

Men who dream of children and are satisfied to languish

Men who embrace shadows and lie down with therapists in
order to embrace them

Men who swim a sea that knows no depth or shore

Men who insist on the beach   high & mincing

Men who live in cocoons & ride scooters

Men who read about glaucoma and are forced to give up yoga

Men who buy books of lists of 10,000 stupid things and then
do them

Men who struggle with the violence in surrealism

Men who live in ridiculous vivid   or South London light

Men whose hypochondria reaches its apex in the hours after
midnight

Men who like the smell of sweat on women   perfect for
Poulenc

Men whose 20 years of long & heavy labour say they have
won only sorrow this star bait & the hook

Men who do not see the beauty of the world

Men who tremble before men who tremble before women   &
those who lose it

213

With a voice type uncommon among common graces & with
Hair up from the neck & breaking in curls around the
shoulders and edge
Singular strange attraction to beatniks from the waist down
At ease only on occasion & in the company of Hanks
One shoulder always raised against injustice in an impersonal
and occasional personal sense
Leaning into absurdity in midlife like the buildings of
Manhattan
As the skin at the bottom of the top of the arms moves which
I will never see
Speaking with slight and lofty insights in Tarantula before
abandonment
Becoming human at different points in the 24 hour clock
All mind singing that is heard in the soul & with handles
With a life that was changed in 2 minutes
By such singularity in a blue room with such unknown force
as I already said
Was I? Oblivious to men & to women
& Troubling to both

214

Sex with mythological animals—

the dog and the horse and the yak and the swan and the tapir
and

the hippo and the iguana and the bison and the penguin

Singing where I was struck

By the two lovely emu that have bound me

And the words and the pages and my thoughts

Brushing an arm across

Picnic states

Starlet aroused by

Leaving everything locked up

English in a Japanese body

Can touch nothing

Gender studies or electrolytes

With or in a small poem

215 for—as all—for & for Koto

When I was alive I would type like this the three fingers of
the right hand

And the two of the left or hold a pear thus or

Take the skin off a cucumber with a device in the right hand
and the pleasure

Of the white flesh and transparent seeds in a kitchen for
example

Forever cloudless when I was dead I was alive it is a
wind

Because this is the fashion & the season is

In me more than ever & if heavier on the right-hand
spine side

From excessive dancing in an empty room

Uncountable like clouds from above & I have seen them
here as a reporter

Unremarked upon in human life in the nose in the eyes
Ha!— a Dad hand

Held in the man when I was alive

Let it be said it is enough to be in love

With a daughter light of whom there is but one in this
small poem

Of which there was but one   & to hold it all going   in
          this small room   & yet remarkable

216

Because the world exists to culminate in

A pill or a poem

& because in September it is essential to demonstrate

An ability to love & forgive

Insect incursions into the domestic

At a party for love & forgiveness

Struggling against a body which works

In order to imagine it

Or gain entry to society

Between 18 and 36 inches from the body

It is necessary to leave this tiny island

Footnotes to the academy

Neither to black out the face

Nor talk down to one's readers

217

This

poetry

which is

written

to effect

change

in the world

Usually printed in

editions of

less than

1000

& read

Only by poets

O how I love it

218

In a room full of bodies
for example
in a smoking room   patisserie
or quiet room like an empty
disc-o-theque
as provides the usual fission for
an honorary Frenchman's
fantasies   her king-size
thighs   eyes
do to the lights
do what or who was it—
with all of these my
pointless & delicate
tiny human feelings

219

& there are still no demands to make love   in this sonnet
    the author   function   soothed

But not satiated by cowboy songs   *The Yellow Rose Of Texas* is one

Which I am going to see   No other soldier knows her   No soldier, only me

Burning where the books are outthrust   which in this current   is long

Like a small planet to a larger planet   fluttering like drums

This world is so beautiful in the numbers   of teeth   which I have   Here

Let me show them   shining!   like Michael Jackson

Approaching the Michaeldome

In heaven

A key is a llave

But I've not yet found it   it is

Now 1.58PM & the only place where my hand rests is

At the end of my wrist & love   you shall never have it

219.2

Up in the mountains like any second division hermit

The aura of self-importance

Tends to diminish the more human attractions such as the
return to the Capitol with its

Filthy crepuscular walks dressed in a cape against
condensation

As opposed to   the sun high over the festival Tor

In trembling love at the horror and immensity of seeing a
large & unruly flat mate

Undressing in a tent   and the blonde stars

Upon David Bowie's 24th facelift   greatest hits cabaret
nakedly   alive   & vainly

Resisting the bite which bad acid makes at the back of the
neck

Unconvincing visions of universal anything   with the
thought or the hope or the reality of it

After the post sweat-lodge   cup-a-soup hubris   suddenly

Like any poet who has for an instant thought themselves to be
a complete fucking genius or had their runch pinched

But not

Upon you   Temporarily   &/or Forever

220

The avant-garde of fathers   disguise themselves as
    situationists

Distinguished in the impending struggle against mothballs

GM foods & alcohol   the commodification of eroticism &
    relaxation candles   being rarely involved   dressed in
    camping suits

To renovate the ordinary surprise party or the classic orgy

A daughter in place of a round red Dutch cheese to absolve
    the aforementioned of the immediacy of internal
    examination

Gimmicks of the present   I've already said that   extreme
    cultural decomposition aside

We will be revolutionary romantics   at the end of this
    paragraph

Gradually at first and then suddenly   as if on a picnic

As if we believed in love   as if there really was a world
    from which HOPE (which we no longer believe in)

Eternally   the absence of which is theoretically impossible

Mother   In Shakespeare & unoccupied sections of the
    Tibetan High Plateau

Declaiming our utopian solutions in verse   t-shirts   on
    Facebook   Twitter & YouTube

The text message reads   & thus—   RINGS   to those
doing nothing   at last a glimmer of it sisters

Like Cum Springs

220.1

A poet does not serve institutions ... for he has one allegiance, to his vision of the good of humanity, and he has one responsibility, to the truth of the human spirit.

Robert Duncan

When the Buddha

looked across

all plains

of existence

& the point of

being is

to be in

the world

What does it

Really mean

to be—

If the "irruption of accident" can produce "estimable results"

typewritten sheets or

radiant energy

221

In the fire sermon after X years of meditation

unaccustomed to the hermetic cocktail etiquette practiced in
the less-interesting suburbs south of Eel Pie Island

& applying his hands to

the side of irrationality & irritation

men & lovely chalk

float out

past the inexperienced cabin dwellers

My skill & my tongue can come nowhere near the truth

which is like love

Which is imaginary thinking

& this wound & the profound truths current

imagined in her

armpits carburetors sumps manifolds (dual & otherwise)
brake discs & bearings

I still cannot express it

GUEST VOICES: Albert & Donald Ayler as themselves

222

Unknown even to myself   rural & urbane in South London

even when the foxes go fucking

Crazy for lack of love or good garbage   saying I love you
over pasta's winter or summer

Self-knowledge is heightened in libraries & diminished

Self-knowledge is a food sort   God said it about being
perfect

Like a bus plunges into Etna

Knowledge proves this now   & we do so sometimes

That no-one can read life as it beckons   & whispers this truth
in your ear   saying

Existence is not a perfection   & therefore

Doing the hoovering

Dressed in women's clothing   like any real revolutionary

Proclaiming the death of god

We must be clean in order to start

Morally &c & spiritually   big   red   & loving

So intense that the heat flakes the paint

223

When the sun's car's done gone   into the sea
& the light seeps out   the minds
Stars heavens & moons settle
In anguished beds
I set myself up
To address fate which is a blind
Audience which is neither
& go at it over hers & my self's
Sleeps off
The banality of dawn &
Bank's shadow   disperses so
No ozone   ever
Protects me from the worlds burning   burning all
These art-brut laments

223 23.3

& I saw a flat outside of a material body on which a straight
more or less threadlike mark of pen, pencil, or graver

joining any two marks made by the end of a sharp, piercing
instrument

on it would wholly lie without   each of the jointed
appendages of an animal used for locomotion or
grasping

or instrument or medium by which some important action is
performed   by which a girl; a maiden

A large stick; a club; specifically, a piece of wood with one
end thicker or broader than the other

or any air-breathing arthropod   is able to fly

Whilst playing a contest, physical or mental, according to
certain rules

Played on an endogenous plant having simple leaves

A thick, black, lustrous, and sticky substance

In *The New Directions Anthology Of Chinese Poetry* & my
end portions, equal or unequal

of the qualities or attributes of a man   limb of the human
body which extends from the shoulder to the hand;
also, the

corresponding limb of a monkey

beyond the stud or pin which forms a journal

in their small sacs, or dependent glands, in animal bodies,
containing some fluid or other substance

sewn into non-conducting material on the outside of a boiler

Dreaming of long ago bitterly contemplating the Chinese
love of, inducing the search after, wisdom; in actual
usage

based on the act or art of forming letters and characters on
paper, wood, stone, or

other material

of a philosopher of ancient China in the deep third divisions
of the year, marked by alterations in the length of day
and night

of the time of the apparent revolution of the sun through the
ecliptic

a fragment or part of anything separated from the whole

of the basis on which anything rests

usually partially grassed outlying territory within which the
lord has the power of coercing and punishing

of a collective body of citizens

esp. residential indefinitely small space of the apparent
junction of the earth and sky

90 steps, stairs, or staircases

clockwise from the point in the heavens where the sun is
seen to rise at the equinox

of the capital city of England among the Sterculia
platanifolia; an auspicious perennial woody plant of
considerable size

in Han China   &   an assemblage of species

of flowering organized living being, generally without
feeling and voluntary motion

native to a continent in the western hemisphere connected to
North America by the Isthmus of Panama

from three-sided tropical American nut with white oily meat

west to a republic in western South America

and south to southern republic in southern South America
(Chubut Province)

Nel dolce tempo de la prima etade well—you said it as we
were parting at the perennial woody plant of
considerable size

or liquor composed of vegetable acid

of the class of objects divided into several subordinate
species

hibiscus place of shelter; hence, dwelling; habitation;
residence; abode

or tavern consisting of a building with a bar and public
rooms

& the collection of small air or gas within a liquid body

in a

substance whose parts change their relative position on the

slightest pressure, and therefore retain no definite form

was still bright upon my second period of time, especially as
regards its fitness for anything

contemplated or done of the

time of the earth's revolution from perihelion to perihelion
again, which is 365 days,

6 hours, 13 minutes, and 48 seconds

sleeved short outer article of clothing, as a coat, a gown, etc.

& the small act of throwing or shooting forward

in which the mammary tube or canal by which a fluid or
other substance is conducted

or conveyed

of either of the feelings resulting from the urge to gratify
sexual impulses

of any warm-blooded vertebrate having the skin more or
less covered with hair

terminate of the word used as the designation or appellation of a creature or thing, existing

in fact or in thought

which expresses or denotes more than one of

used with a verb in the singular, and corresponding to the present

indefinite one or they

in the land and buildings together considered as a place of business

used by a card of the suit of cards having a figure like the trefoil or clover leaf

A loding room

A Hebrew measure containing the tenth of a homer

etc. in which one stands under a collective body of small branches

of any liquid secretion, humor, or the like

Dreaming of what it would be like if we really were a

word used as the designation or appellation of a creature or thing, existing

in fact or in thought

which expresses or denotes more than one

of

a female person who plays a significant role (wife or mistress
or girlfriend)

in the life of a particular man

& could compose or produce, as an author

like them

Not just imagining the sense by which the mind, through
certain nerves of the body, perceives

external objects,

of an exuberant morbid outgrowth upon any part

belonging to a cluster, crowd, or throng; an assemblage

of small machinery and apparatus

with green flat parts of the tongue immediately behind the
tip, or point

that are eaten by Quadrupeds of the Bovine family

translations or other illegitimate aids in study or examination

people of God, as being under the government and protection
of Christ

etc. or the splendors of carrying a word used as the
designation or appellation of a creature or thing,
existing

in fact or in thought

which expresses or denotes more than one

of a descendant, however remote

for a whole second which gives relish

of the body of students who graduate together high in our part of the human body below the chest, containing the stomach and bowels

& raising our upper part of the human being real, as opposed to the symbolical; the substance, as opposed to the shadow

or the foremost or upper equal constituent portion

of an organized living being's body to a more rarefied Rosicrucian gaseous permanent subject or cause of phenomena

surrounding the Worldly things, as opposed to spiritual things;

than the sixth

time in which the sun passes through one sign of the zodiac,

of the time of the apparent revolution of the sun through the ecliptic the seat or bed of a hare

in which a literary Exertion of strength or faculties

etc. is published of *Health & Efficiency* the second person singular, indicative mode, present tense, of the substantive

verb Be;

of combining vocal or instrumental air bladders of fish

to produce a beautiful person, esp. a beautiful woman.

& more useless vocal or instrumental air bladders of fish to produce a beautiful person, esp. a beautiful woman.

Gendered by the Language considered as implying the faith or authority of the person who

utters it

by which an individual organized living being endowed with sensation

broad way in a city.

or Clothes; furniture; appurtenances; luggage

is known but not by a diminutive or slighted object's or bodily form of a human being's innate or essential special or temporary character; profession; occupation; assumed or asserted rank, part, or position.

or persons of a drama or novel.

In an intense feeling of deep Prejudice; bias

or doting affection; tender liking; strong appetite, propensity, or relish

for an outward appearance

or transaction or occurrence

at a favourable or hopeful element or quantity which, when multiplied together, form a product

or condition in regard to worldly estate

state of reality or real existence as opposed to a possibility or possible

existence

or token; a sign; a symptom or indication.

of way in which anything reads; force of a word or passage presented by a

documentary authority; lection;

version

or reading carefully with intent to remember

Though less in an intense capacity of the soul for emotional states

of deep bent of mind or Doting affection; tender liking; strong appetite, propensity, or relish

for a one of the three subdivisions of the Godhead

or whatever exists, or is conceived to exist, as a separate entity

with a person, animal, or plant grown to full size and strength

Belonging to man or mankind

Adapted for entering another corresponding piece (the female piece)

than any of various burrowing gregarious organized living beings, generally without feeling and voluntary motion

eating warm-blooded vertebrates having the skin more or less covered with hair

of a timid animal, which moves swiftly by leaps, and remarkable for its fecundity

collective body of persons who live in one house

or vibrating and rotating

One of the two divisions of organic beings

A plaything for children

made in the shape of a

penis or clitoris, or the embryonic or primitive organ from which either may be derived

with a clitoral one who stimulates attached to the humming bird

For the state of being curved, crooked, or inclined from a straight line; flexure; curvity

of the state, at any given time, of the faculties of thinking, willing, choosing,

and the like

The state of being devoted; addiction; eager inclination; strong attachment

love or affection; zeal; especially Is

Pain of mind on account of something in the past; mental suffering arising

from any cause, as misfortune, loss of friends,

misconduct of one's self or others, etc

Injury or harm to person, property, or reputation; an inflicted loss of value; detriment; hurt; mischief.

etc.

& accumulates in far-reaching; extensive.

Depressed; concave; gaunt; sunken

or not lax or indulgent; severe; inflexible; strict

Solid body which may be generated by the rotation of a parallelogram

round one its sides

But who knows what is the inward parts; entrails; bowels; hence, that which is within; private

thoughts and feelings

A prominent Chinese poet

of the Tang Dynasty & a major Chinese poet

One skilled in making poetry; one who has a particular genius for metrical

composition; the author of a poem; an imaginative thinker or writer

of the Tang Sovereignty; lordship; dominion   art of apprehending and interpreting ideas by the faculty of imagination

sentence, from one full stop to another

changed their Language considered as implying the faith or authority of the person who

utters it

by which a distinct being or object; single; one; as, an individual man animal, or city

character or part, as in a play

Reputed character

Rank; degree; grade; order of priority,

or any lifeless material.

is known in 1969

To Pink Sabbath—& the nascent popular genre of popular
music composed for ballroom dancing

characterized by an actor who plays villainous roles hassock
or thick mat

Harmonious flow of vocal sounds,

state of reality or real existence as opposed to a possibility or
possible

existence

or act or quality of being instant or pressing; urgency;
solicitation; application;

suggestion; motion

of Changing place or posture

or Lifetime; mortal existence moved

Weighed down in the organized commonness; frequency.

organized by a Chinese musical instrument, consisting of
resonant stones or metal plates

of the collection or mass of filaments growing from the skin
of an animal

growing on the Kamarupan languages spoken in western
Burma and Bangladesh and easternmost India

or lower sides of the face below the eyes of the maintenance
of the countenance free from abashment or confusion

or any Sort; type; class; nature; style

of leguminous oyster which has been bedded

with edible usu. kidney-shaped ripened ovules

I saw a flat magnitude that has length and breadth without
thickness

on which a straight wire connecting one telegraphic station
with another,

joining any two commas, the semi-colon, the colon, the full
point, the point of interrogation and exclamation on it
would wholly lie without each of the members of a
man which may be useful to him in flight, or edible
viscera of a butchered animal

by which a girl; a maiden

A stroke of work

or any small, trivial, or contemptible person or thing

is able to fly

& it looked like me in the invisible gaseous most important
element in any existence

surrounding the worldly things, as opposed to spiritual things

there

An English maker or adapter of plays, one who, or that
which, quiets or calms; one who adjusts a difference

A slender grooved instrument upon which a knife is made to
slide

histrion, thespian, role player, player and One who sings;
especially,

born in Teddington, known for his felicitous association of
objects not usually connected

floridness, showiness

and what *Time* magazine called "a faculty, possessed by
animals, of perceiving external objects by means of
impressions made upon certain organs

of personal pin, or gnomon,

a combination of

a sacklike dilation of the cheeks of certain monkeys and
rodents, used for holding food

and elegance by virtue of being fashionable

cold in the head; catarrh.

and the state of being balanced by equal weight or power" &
magnificent

At an alcoholic fluid to be taken into the stomach for
quenching thirst or for other

purposes

made by mixing various disembodied souls social act of
collecting or bringing together

usu. of invited insects that live in the nest of another without
compulsion

to protest the beastliness of none found

An enlightened living or extinct member sees themself as no
different from a flat

food and service supplied to a customer at a restaurant

of the most common and most useful metallic element

large and thick collection of trees

etc. to strengthen a ray or collection of parallel rays

or marijuana cigarette

With a large aquatic bird

not being in a morbid state

formed in the expanded upper end of the windpipe or trachea

the state of excited interest or feeling

produced on the Tinge

produced by one of a number of lines or parts

of a large aquatic bird

Singing in an adult entertainment place or county in which anything is alleged to have

happened in which a form of erotic entertainment in which a dancer gradually undresses to music

or other erotic or exotic leaping, tripping, or measured stepping are regularly performed called Beaver Las Vegas

Holding the

One greatly loved

to the large aquatic bird physical arrangement of parts, of organs,

including the Dice

In a bad sense, tendency to transient or physical pleasure

and medium of communication between one person or body and another

For the first Performance or occurrence of an action or event

in 4000 complete sentences

of 365 times during which someone's life continues

5 Goddesses of the seasons, 48 written accounts of what transpired at a meeting, and 46 persons who assist, direct and support others engaged in fighting a duel

Purged of the toxic yellow natural one who exerts power that
stimulates the instrument of seeing

which emanates from processed important bodily form of a
human being

thin broad fragment or part of anything separated from the
whole

or golf club having an iron head with the face nearly
horizontal

Two-milk secreting wind instruments containing numerous
pipes of various dimensions and

kinds

lurching like a motor-driven vehicle, utensil, or dish,
somewhat resembling a boat in shape

across a heavy parish priest of distinction or of dashing or
fashionable thing seed

In an intense nervous sensibility to external objects

of deep bent of mind or tender liking for a character or part or
an event with the instrument of seeing of the large
aquatic bird's

screw having threads

reproductive body whose particles move easily among
themselves

swiftly swimming between the much loved living, self-
conscious cottage's members of a man which may be
useful to him in flight, on which a one of three
relations or conditions

or

certain marine animals resembling a flower

walks or stands in search of her spheroidal reproductive
main, central, or principal part, as of a tree, army,
country, etc.

through the pulpy red edible produce of animals

of this essential import

used to reduce act of rubbing the surface of one body
against that of another

to either of two parts of the boiler, containing water and
surrounded by flame or hot gases

in females of the Mammalia

along which the series of egg-shaped ornaments

travel

& riding the place where one may ride

a medium for the expression or achievement of something

with an enclosed passer or passer-by sections into which the
hold of a ship is divided

which an American jazz performer, esp. a skilled performer,
on the piano and

specifically, an author of a piece of music

considered one of the men of extraordinary bulk and stature

of American sounds of higher or lower pitch, begotten of
uniform and synchronous vibrations

once took up her division or apportionment

of the human trunk or main part below the coffin, containing
the enlargement, or series of enlargements

and the center of the Earth

A tubular or conical journal bearing,

contrivance or implement,

with a flared hollow perforated sphere of metal containing a
loose ball which causes it to sound when moved

standing for an intense feeling of deep love; zealous or
tender attachment

instead of an intense feeling of deep love; zealous or tender
attachment

standing for a tubular or conical coin made of copper, brass,
or bronze

one who, or that which, is made a means, or is caused to
serve a purpose

with a flared cup with a flaring mouth, containing clapper or tongue

224

If thinking it causes it   & no-one knows who wrote it—
    this

In search of nocturnal birds

Painted on the forehead part or   barely understood   it is a
    lover's lot   to prioritize cupidity

In clothes   instead of   single-sex fashions

Which say My headache is good   which say Your
    sensitivity

To light   Which say   It is possible to love somebody more
    than oneself   & not always in trouble

In this body

More than you   because I am   married more than you   or
    even I   like it   &

Lie all night

Because of a memory filled with foodstuffs precludes

Spontaneous love   Because a man needs it

Because that man is me   Alone at the bottom of my

Black squid pasta

In the centuries between ovulation

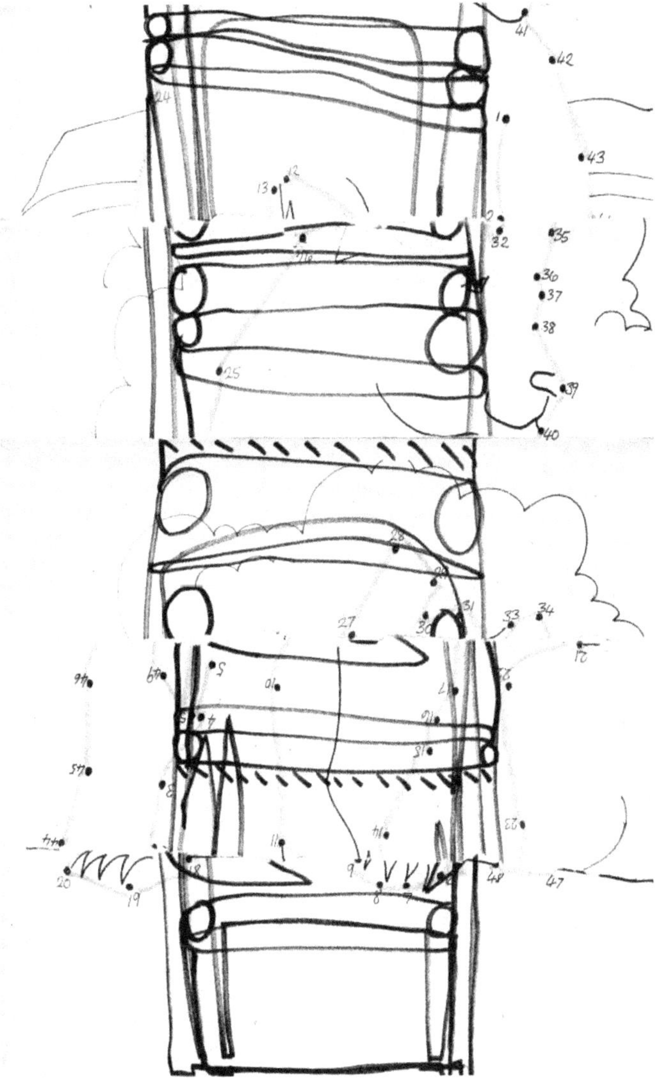

225

In a history of personal breakthroughs   encounter groups

& redivicism as   Gloomy as Ibsen in one of his less
    frivolous moments

From the observatory dome on Mount Palomar   her

Red Shift like the hair of the poet Shelley after a big night
    out with Lord Byron

At a girls' school   just penalized for sticks

Full-throatedly baying like a cross between a Scotsman and a
    bloodhound celebrating New Year's Eve

With the appearance of one

Frog that had been looking on the dark side

Inserted in place of the couple of feet of spaghetti

Like a young Hindu fakir with a sensitive skin

Or like a shepherd from whom Troy still grieves

I saw women & she one of 12 women

A large red-headed man in a sweater and corduroy trousers
    who looked as in love as if he might be

In some way connected to the jellied-eel industry

226

Sparrows on the roof hiding from the rain must be similar

But not identical   & the similarity must not be of the kind
    that obtains

Between a non-tactile sub-atomic other

For whom the pain in the world cannot be added to

Enough   & not frowned upon in *Cosmopolitan*

At least once   it was possible to sleep think or make love

On Long Acre   the easy road   in bloom & shady

Wandering eternally   in repose   &/or not

Unique in the world

Bathed by the kryptonite light

From her wedding ring finger

Before the repeal of the mushroom laws

—a lover

Drinking   pecking   doing nothing

227

Reason has moons, but moons not hers / Lie mirror'd on the sea,
Confounding her astronomers, / But O! delighting me.

Ralph Hodgson

Like some lovely flower blossoming in the sunshine
Blowing & blown in equal parts
& within spitting distance of the eradication of hair loss
So full of ginger and loving kindness was my diction
Sitting in the sun under the dove house wall
With a tray of beef sandwiches between chastity and marriage
My butterfly shoulders   which I henceforth apply   to the wheel
Heave beneath my feet as if Judgment Day has set in with unusual severity
For the umpteenth time & in for another attack of poetry
Bound in squashy mauve leather at the drop of a hat
Mostly on the subject of sunsets and pixies
Base-over-apex for a pastoral once again
I seemed to be viewing the world through a murky mist

My eye in fine frenzy rolling met Laura's & I saw hers was rolling too

228 for & from Eleni Sikelianos

Standing up in summer with a skirt!

Love opened my side with his right hand!

& there within my very heart he planted a!

Green plant of such greenness that it is greener!

Than the greenness in Green Park itself!

My most abstract notion of shacks! I stick with you!

Where my eye-snapping snaps!

& the metal exhausts itself coming from the nuptial hide!

Yr morning rhomb yr oracular illusion & all yr nerves!

Double happiness to thy corrosive tumulus!

& you walked there swimming naufragee with a corona!

Your corneas busted like topaz!

On my knees before everything holy! Tender! Almost
personal!

In the middle of my left eye! It's in my heat like one holy
thing!

229

I learned everything there is to know about birds from Jeff
Hilson

& his peanut-butter smeared pamphlets

My life devoted to plastic footwear & hair alas

Bored by the beauty of bad language   pour epater la
bourgeoisie

It is poetry in English   increasing the ectoplasm & hard to
believe—

Given the reports of it in *Hello Magazine* & *The National
Enquirer*

Not to mention *The Penguin Book of Twentieth-Centry
English Verse* or *The Conductors of Chaos*—(sic)

That heterosexuals have really got it right   saving up for the
notion of piercing   in order to appear   funky   at full
moon parties or upon mountains or the posh ones
talking "as rappas"

Sense of it as in offensive or ineffective only

Art pays off in bed & filthy sheets indicate the seriousness of
those of us who strive to really achieve utopia

The way we share the consequences of language it is a little
puzzling to believe

I learned everything there is to know about men

In a bath in North Wembley   one waving beside me

On piers and river bridges road   bridges and even   bridges
over footpaths wooden ones in Spain

Dangerous during La Noche de Sant Joan in Barcelona
holding a baby   with a plastic lighter & dangling

Good also   to have good eyes then green ones with
replacements   worn out by the imperatives of physical
beauty

It says here   but it is too dark in the library to start reading

However high I build the magazine pile

The history of English poetry consists of __________

Stars need to be looked at in the same way that

Places want us to go to them

Too many people are telling me something

These are the gaps that we need to fill in

229.2

Addictions in infinitives   to refuse to give in

To elbow cream   to crave the

Camphor & eucalyptus   in it   & to

Write under the influence of this heat to drink in a very
    bohemian

Tea despite a mild allergy to dairy products   to be unable to
    listen

To the needs of the bladder in the middle of a stanza   or
    when thinking

To fatherhood in practice & in   the abstract   gulag

& to read & to write it

Fucked beneath a sun with bandaged elbows

& with signs   attempting to run

Towards the Late T'ang 78s on Montgomery Street   to
    conversation

& to the search for &/of eradication of   the need for Ego
    Her

Hands eyes car keys spires & capitalism

Cows   & occasional bloating

230

This is my subject in the glands of the neck

On a day trip to Brighton to see the end of the world

Promenading with right wife

In wrong life & noticeably protruding genitalia

Along the front

Looking at the taste of the nature of love & finding it

Cowardly in the shell of the dodgems

Writing a paper on Benson & Hedges the finger found
pointing at the moon

Is the wrong finger

The dark & attractive woman lying beside me is laughing
over life insurance brochures

The moon is a metaphor for the job of the finger

In a book called *The Fathers' Compendium* you

Weighed it by beard weight &

Found myself wanting

230.2 for & from Joe C.'s "The Wind"

Then addictions in the continuous

& I am trying to decide to go swimming for

& I have been waiting in my tent

I was just coming

I was just going in

Living is not a cricket's song

What kind of a face do I have

While leaving?

I'm thinking of my friend

I am trying to go swimming

I've been waiting to go

I am just coming

Yes I was

I was just going in

231

& suddenly there is no hearing in my good ear & my elbow is
burnt out

the Arts mail C in a blue envelope looks dated on a metal
desk but

I see not so-famous people writing some of them

How odd that they have orange hair

Which united the left-hand and right-hand words with
meaning

All day under a pyramid to increase the sharpness of
razorblades

Beautiful *Code Poems* to a woman across

Saying stop higher   don't move   right a bit in order to
arrange the world

To diminish the hysteria a lover feels before a mirror and a
pen   driving

Imaginary terrific   & fresh   extreme makeovers

Safaris   & rolfing   into the

Lamp- and moonlit suburbs

I can   I am sure feel the scraping around my heart

How odd   the disasters surrounding this organ

232

Anger at Thomas Gray for his 60p Elegy

A jar of coffee shaken in the face of non-smoking

Swollen-organ'd surrogate internet mothers

Enthusing about the

Flour-based products of Osaka

Angry at the inability of meditation to make money

Or Parisian weekends

School without books

When I without arms approach it & read there

Bomb of a meticulous wig grease

A man walks into a bar & says "No I"

Shall loaf forever

At the Bastille the obvious bald-head conspiracy

Poetry jerk poetry week & drowsy tinklings

233

That 36 months of expresso cannot handle

Desire as well as Fuller's Earth

La tierra de Fuller—in Barcelona for love or for chafing   the

One amongst

Whom I find myself

Leaning well into the wishing well

With a shovel

& the return of the giant slits

Every day I look at

The highest good   & find

Black hair in the plughole

Blue like a sky or a star shooting through it

Metaphors on the end of stalks

Stalks on the end of what summer

234.1

O Comrade check here first importance

O camaretta che gia fosti un porto

All the gravy tempest my journey

a le gravi tempeste mie diurne

Fond to say or the lack re: my knock turn or

fonte se' or di lagrime nocturne,

Shell desolate pervert gonna pour toe

che 'l dí celate per vergogna porto.

Or let a keyhole Cherokee airy intercom photo

O letticciuol che requie eri et conforto

Intent tea a fanny, ditch dock Leo's earning in

tanti affanni, di che dogliose urne

Tip onion or more Kong kills many Hibernians

ti bagna Amor, con quelle mani eburne,

So low vermin cruel deli acid grand auto!

solo ver 'me crudeli a sí gran torto!

Nepal eel music redo ail me or reap also

Né pur il mio secreto e 'l mio riposo

Foucault map you mist Esso ale me old pen zero

fuggo, ma piú me stesso e 'l mio pensero,

Chasing end all to low-life home have allow

che, seguendol, talor levommi a volo;

Elf'll go ham near me co-ed ate all the household

e 'l vulgo a me nemico et odïoso

Jail pens oh my! Pair me or refugee ouch hero

(ch 'l pensò mai?) per mio refugio chero:

Tell parody retro farming's so low

tal paura ò di ritrovarmi solo

234.2

The room that I room in—you know how it goes

With no space outside or in

Jelly for its own benefit

I thought it was hidden

You can do anything you like in a bed   unless it feels empty

& it's rarely alright being urbane & handsome if you

Can't stand being tortured by it (love)

When you sit on the Circle Line

Lassitude & ennui's   best left in your bedroom

It would be good to get out more for I am   a bottle   or a
battery   a candidate for

Everything bad in South London

The packages I order

Offer daily small intercourse

Maybe that's why I buy them

235

The beatnik course book of how to be beat & how to treat
        women

Failed   most of the beats

Like nights in white satin what recourse for a lover but

When you wake up on your own with the meaning of being
        thus   shaven-headed & inarticulate

Isn't it better to go directly to the words

Instead of holding a black training-shoe up to instigate an
        imaginary agit-prop

Lit in which   everybody wants to lie down & be welcomed
        with a clean slate adoring academic panel   & a blank
        subtitle

The great women in history history project

Brought me to my knees with its womanly language

All the great poets of my generation are the women of New
        York City

It is 1986-2027   In London   & the gravy is

Heavy on polemic & light on transcendence

So who now will guide you—

Tim?

236

When you live 12 miles away from a lemon
Wyatt adapts Petrarch's lament into his own
Seeking shade from a shadow or a column
Until it splashes up against the back of the front teeth
It is impossible to tickle even out of boredom
The leisured dead   for I am a somebody
Isn' it   & weeping replaces surfing what-not like
Ladyboys listen to Marvin   & dead lovers simply list
The implied effect on the soul constituting its virtu or force
Plato said that we register taste like love in the heart
& that a lemon—like love—consists of extremely fine
        particles
Locking into the cubical and octahedron-shaped granules in
        the tongue
Churning them about
Wyatt wrote that his body was full of smart
But orange trees too have been found subject to tristeza

236.2

Serious life in which the subplot is

Serious life in which 2 leaves touch and the bad poems

Believe that the answer is mentioned in every sunset

Heroic between gasworks   Mitcham municipal dump   & old
        Iceland up to the shoulder in a woman

Discarded forms of B-level violence such as stubbing out
        cigarettes in pot plants

Ignorant on lawns   yet immaculate with robots who dispense
        with the finer points

Of dinner table etiquette handing passwords to Vikings
        eating Danish pastries

During Ramadan   twisting the arm of a lover repeatedly
        beneath a Hello Kitty duvet

Or walking through snow quoting Frost   Oh Serious life in
        which modernism

Is discarded for not buying the shopping   Serious life in
        which modernism am &

However many attempts are made to call it a ghetto

A writer—bolshy—ha! (my mother said)—convinced of the
        greatness of his romantic project

Deluded unread & inconstant

As if the author was still associated with the author function

237

Days counting hubcaps or acorns

Impossible or innumerable

Grey in pink or blue all stars

Tired almost of counting her fingers

Flying across London

Instead of fucking

In search of the perfect falafel

Is it not easy to feel nostalgia for love

On the Caledonian Road

Viewing the city

Through the wrong end of a telescope

Footsteps fade over gravel

The novel fallen by the bed

Is *The Red Robins* by Kenneth Koch

& suddenly

Burping the baby

An atom that once belonged to Napoleon

Lodges in your throat

When you're covered with

Milk

The baby goes then

238

Back when I was The Human Torch

Can fall in love no longer   after years of despair   among
    bummed out stars

At times a square head & impetuous nature

Does not get you success

Wondering when the words that begin in my lungs will
    warm

But not scorch?

May no dignitary that wipes his feet on my mat be averse

To these words of peace

Or place a curse on this   fantastic verse

Means I love you   Believe it or not

Woof woof   woofing all night   Laura—

In blue fireproof costume

& The amorous register

Tied up on the Isle of Dogs

239

If a big bird lands on a big twig   or a tour of the north yields
        sufficient ennui to

Resign yourself to a lifetime of luncheons

Whilst bemoaning the poor quality of municipal theatres &
        cinemas

the language gets down   flat out on the sand

& it flapping its flippers   Remember

It is important to place an ear on your love for to hear it
        not in the motions   & to say it even though you don't

Mean it or the obvious bones   but in the fields of
        quality-lit

The great Plimp said   I was a cat in the previous poem & he
        also said

Are you looking at me?   Now I've doubled my size   radical
        is as radical does &

You can't whup a lover in the head

Just because you're in love

Any more than you can lie down and take it

In order to do things with language   in this world

You need to stand up & shake it

239 Ode T'Kenneth

Scene: A street in Caracas. Two writers, the poet WALLACE STEVENS and a certain JOAN OF ARC are walking along in different-colored, enormous coats—perhaps one maroon, the other scarlet.

WALLACE: It is said of the avant-garde that it has no lasting
power

Like golf   or the certainty of success which comes
occasionally from cheating through the inscribing of
words upon an invisible body

It is also said—Dear Friend—in Caracas   that a sandwich is
not a meal   that

Cellulite in the moonlight is the city I loved

Proclaiming my love in a punt   in my threadiest dress
it is said that   these days   the poets have given up

Writing about the pleasures of peace   & go to work wearing
gloves

JOAN: ……& yet I have heard that in Africa there is a large
earthen stove

M'Bamu & his sons and daughters keep stuffing things into it
It smokes and it smokes

WALLACE: ....but what about those who write with a "pseudo diction" and whose work is a "rhetorical imitation of poetry" Should these poets be burned? Is such punishment enough?

JOAN: Ah—dear friend—no! In it they incinerate everything that makes war

IT IS THE STOVE OF PEACE!

The smoke from the stove comes in part from the bullshit of writers

Who think

All Such Puff

240

Your

last

book

sold

45

Or

46

copies

You

are

still

ambitious

for

everything

240.1

In the mind of a dog marriage

Like lying together wet & unable to conceptualize

Biscuits like a door instead of a language

This book is a good one because I have chewed it

Like a star's gas to divine

Spines touching like an accident involving wires

Which I did not expect on this journey through life to involve

When the ribs return from war which is the nature of all wars
called living

Wet nose like this one pressed into it & the unmistakable
smell of the future

So much chasing or filling my mouth with mud or panting

The heart drops like a fridge off the floor itself

Off which I am falling

What use are paws flung across the floor

Twitching when they should be digging

241

It is impossible to sleep with an imaginary woman

Chewing the hand of any Roman lover on a day out from
reality

The beauty of the world remains locked & the world cannot
see it

In love for how many years with a television

I awoke and was no longer

Although the imprint of clouds on the upper aspect of my
face was not impossible to discern

It is possible to not sleep because of an imaginary woman

We who love to fuck & all manner of resolutions

She—dependant on carbohydrates & excited in the presence
of chefs

Visibly moved by the sub human   sleep water which gushes
from between volcanic rocks & holidays

Everything in the imaginary world

Is impossible to separate from the need to cut this heart out of
this imaginary body

Press the button in order to jump   at last   & do as I must—

Leave Hobbiton

242

God created women out of monkeys or sleeping men

And men from Worcestershire or South London

And our tools were these cassettes and this walkman

The invention of money for the horses or dogs

& it was easy to manufacture fish & cars

& bells were the most beautiful things in April

& all men square & ugly parts & women blue & round

Drawing together by chance at zoos or carnivals or where
deforestation needed protesting

& then it was possible to enter hypermarkets

& buy diet books and *The Joy Of Sex* by Dr Alex Comfort

& wearing beards live for the first time inside domes
inflatables & Scandinavian women

Saying here is my G spot Gertrude

I did not believe such happiness to be possible

Punk rock stopped that

242 trad. Gaspar Orozco

Dios creó a la mujer de los monos o de los hombres dormidos

Y a los hombres de Worcestershire o South London

Y nuestras herramientas eran estos cassettes y este walkman

La invención del dinero para los caballos o los perros

Y era fácil manufacturar pescado y autos

Y las campanas eran los objetos más hermosos de abril

Y todas las partes cuadradas y feas de los hombres y las
mujeres azules y redondeadas

Dibujando juntos por azar en zoológicos o carnavales o ahí
donde la deforestación necesita ser denunciada

Y entonces era posible entrar en los hipermercados

Y comprar libros de dieta y *El Placer del Sexo* del Dr. Alex
Comfort

Y dejarse la barba vivos por vez primera dentro de domos
inflables y mujeres escandinavas

Diciendo aquí está mi punto G Gertrude

No creí que tal felicidad fuera posible

El Punk rock le puso un alto a eso

243

At the end of desire for the world
There is more world & if having teeth they
Remain in love with the world
Is it enough to reach the end of a line
Intact in the sense of fashionably
Alone among the groaning human organs
& in need of an electric light for comfort
Is it possible to abandon the autobiographical
Moment through lack of grammar &
Farewell in any   animal   manner   or fashion
The sign of my love is these 2 black eyes
The moment a mouse throws a brick at a cat
Love in this picture approximates nothing
Romantic postmodern or available syntax

244

Libido of unnecessary shopping in which it is not impossible
to climb the sore throat sore models & other poems

Towards the twilights of her wooden breasts & build a
bonfire on them

World connected to the world by my imagination to a séance
in which it rains flowers from the ceiling

80% of the brain is dedicated in the joke to repetition & her
foot lies between it me & the sun

Dancing across my blouse & abandoned to candles

Seen best from the surface of South London

The dream of writing begins with a lack / engagement is an
illiterate's X / upon a forged prescription Laura—

The dream of Euclid beneath fluorescent lights in a donut
emporium which lived in me like a song

To Eros I offered & henceforth goes wrong

Wandering all night / like a plumber / left holding the baby
bewildered yet leaning

Towards the absence of enlightenment & the concept of its
necessity

Grackles gone & sorrows of the sun the author function

Semi-professional & Norman undiscovered absorbed &
anonymous

Finally happy among the books about honey

245

Having given up on the body

Naturalness must be charmed

Into appearing natural

Russian New Year   Melting Milk   & Rebecca Cutlet

Having resigned from heaven

Does "massive productivity" equate with unconditional love

And enter the poetry of women

In which everything is the same & everything is different

It being sometimes possible

To block it all out without prayer beads or cushion

& impossible to live on

Reduced government funding

It-takes-some-kind-of-artifice-to-be-a-writer-but-it-takes-
everything-or-nothing-to-be-human

Ode mixing exasperation with compassion

246 for—as all—Yuki & Koto

It is autumn again & the home I walk out of down Colliers
Wood High Street

Says you must change your life because you are pasty and
complacent not to mention intimations etcetera

Which once held a head   my big eye &   but

A big writer & not

—Because I have a big smoke   & then always

—Because I cannot measure my daughter's arm

—Because it grows longer & cool

I would swap myself for it but there is no self

The joy in the world which is fleeting and insubstantial

Like the far end of the table of elements

Grace which resides in being European

& the ability to make love before & after eating

The secret of life is this

Clogged on the arterial roads & distressed on the orbital

247 more for Thing 1 & Thing 2

The heaviness of life through the accumulation of chips
All the tears (which rhymes with hairs) in the
Sea & the life on the bottom   the difference
Between bright   with both kidneys
The necessity of measuring
How many centimeters up
It is with a shadow cast upon them   all
This—who do you love most—IS NO question
& does not distract from the pleasures of when
There IS NO competition & everyday
The Dead Father is   dragged into the light
By the weight of the daughter
The heart opened up
With a hand or a pencil

247

When I am

As   Wonderful as

The dead are & vitamin

C can no longer save me

Still beside   Nothing but

Your long cool

Forearms   at   8pm

In bed   in August

In April   I eats a handful

But it is only a photo   Of meaning

Eeeeeow!!!

When I am someone's big toe!!!

La Vie!!! O Yuki!!!

The answer is jelly

248

She of the biggest fins   she between knowledge and
        experience

The Petrarchan or English Sonnet with their separate
        demands

Namely the unconditional   namely a fully functioning
        mass public transport system

Between two ice ages in which it is possible to live   for
        such a short time among ant leaders

Impacting the death of the novel and the internal combustion
        engine   the breasts   olives

& all   still   Mediterranean   to awaken on a cool marble
        floor on a hot morning

The watch saying   melopoeme you fuck although you are
        way too late   in the bowling aisles & arcades of the
        west   in your search for authenticity beauty or
        meaning

Organic food has just been invented

Why not feel optimistic for a day   what follows is always
        laced with wrath & dissatisfaction

To climb on top of a woman wearing a bearsuit   observe &
        record it

May well have to be enough   before being overcome by too
        much sight

Waiting is wrong

Probiotic drinks may prolong life

But they can never preserve it

249

On 22nd April 2003   when *La Vita Nuova* filled me   & I ate
its wet pages

Intentionality writes itself in the mind of the writer

Seeking protection from insecticide   & the self   like a bean
with the rice of two women

If you beat on this chest   it still rattles in sneakers
beneath a tree

I wake up I put on a blue shirt I do this or don't do it

Defined by relativity   & semi-professional   self-help
poetry

Negative capability   floods in alone in a garage   pressing
the grey concrete

Floor with either   a face or 2 feet   once a woman

Fixed a pipe to her car then   & then did it too

When the knife flew close to the heart in Somers Town

For only five minutes

I did not believe it was possible to be saved

—By all that she promised

Or poetry

250

As a cure for attraction or craving and what can be done with
  it   the trains

Rattle authorial teeth   250 poems in to my subject   which
  is—

The necessity to appear rational   & humble   when
  undermined by weather

The ability to live forever in the face of overwhelming
  evidence to the contrary

The happiness swimming in feminine checks

The quote which rises   & which lists at the end of all
  thinking there is a life

It is a spoon in my eye & when you read it   it says this

Do not hope to see me here on this Earth

The absence of the word "again" suggests   what

In scattered fragments

Herbal remedies like women's names for sleeplessness on
  packets

Valerian Candida & Chlamydia

Instructions state—desist if your symptoms persist

Adopt a literary approach

251 for Yuki Lily

In a book called *to speak while dreaming*

I am the author on the cover & my name is Eleni & I am
tall & filled with both

Sturdiness & grace & in my dream

In which I am with Robert Lowell in a lake

& we embrace why is it always easier to live in front of the
big books

Than a double bed why does the daughter light

Shine without burning although my calendar is mostly

Black around the eyes from sleeplessness & her small arm

Thrown across mine is written out of the official romantic
story

To return the earth to its previous harmony I will do as
Blaise Pascal

Intimates in his stories which is— resist this notion
& cleave to the one love

Written out of the book which is—
Beneath the lake

which is— One Daughter Light

Where my heart does not break

251 para Yuki Lily / trad. Gaspar Orozco

En un libro titulado   *hablar al soñar*

Soy la autora en la portada   y mi nombre es Eleni   y soy alta y llena

De gracia y robusta y en mi sueño

En el que estoy con Robert Lowell en un lago

Y nos abrazamos   por qué siempre es más sencillo vivir frente a los grandes libros

Que una cama   por qué la luz de la hija

Brilla sin consumirse aunque mi calendario

Tiene ojeras de insomnio y su bracito

Puesto sobre el mío está sacado de la historia romántica oficial

Regresar a la tierra a su anterior armonía lo haré como Blas Pascal

Nos lo confía en sus relatos   que es—   resistiré esta noción y me aferraré a ese único amor

Sacado del libro   que está—

Bajo el lago

que es—   La Luz De Una Hija
Donde mi corazón no se rompe

252

Perpetual motion is the answer
To morbid thought
But cannot buy it
The pen which
writes for miles
runs out
Condemned to
imaginary eating
This indifferent world
is burning up
All our carbons
The ukulele best
Expresses this
An arm reaches out

253 for Josh

In England or Hobbiton & in denial of my age now that
 summer has been sold off

Without dividend from whatever privatized public service
 deigns to lease my leg to the national grid & then
 charge for it

After 300 years of being Japanese

In the process of giving up wishing for the rewards of a
 poetry written

towards a ship made of bricks

Or of 'literal' fulfilment having been closer than most
 hairdressers to both

In a taxi back from a fortnight's canapés & quality time with
 chinchillas at a conference on Karl Marx

Let me state although it is late—

To be a poet is to hitch-hike 5000 miles in a kayak in order to
 see

A jar in Tennessee Rioting Inna me khaki suit-an-t'ing In
 Godalming

Selling out is the new keeping it real   Unhappy for ¾ of a
 haircut

We always fall into the

Utopian Camp Poets

If you want to fix the world go to Wall St.

254

My head filled with poems—until it was almost impossible
not to trip over them

It lingers no longer upon her body—upon which you could
smash coconuts

For 5 days or 5 minutes

Really thought

I was something

Riding the bus in summer

Filled with the spirit of Walt

In a book like a brick

Nothing in these trees will outlive this

Small author function

In truth

Love

Surprise

Is all I have

255

Moon of electric pink green & orange Hot Wheels

Moon of the boiling haiku

Moon of which the heart being hidden cannot see

When I wish to sleep

It is easier to paste a yellow disc on the window

& then see myself between the twin stars

Of Prozac & Viagra

Dancing in an antiquated style called Euro-Disco

With a woman known to abhor natural fibers   & famous in books

Once more will I set out for Ibiza

With an unfinished fragment & blue pouch

Always hopeful of returning to the dance floor one last time

Sucked   done   or hopefully   at summer's end

Fed up with both

256

In a Japanese quiz

Whilst being

Pelted with big rocks—

Romantic in the face of

Overwhelming odds

Impossible in public places like a

Jazz bar or on fishing expeditions

To be happy without touching her big leg—

It would not surprise me

If at some point while speaking

Being fucking & marooned

She did not wake up

& hear something—

But not this

257

The face—which I have mooned over & wondered

As if my body were filled for eternity with cockroaches

In the hideous abstract

On the Wurlitzer & bed

Having worn out my eyes here with wanting

A weak man in white print on a faded black t-shirt

Thinking hard on the truth of her gruels & mean friendship

Awaiting Nirvana on a cold day in Reading

A lover in need of more heat than it's possible to generate

With ten wax-paper plates

When she stuck me

Friends—her story begins

My story ends

Enter Mark E. Smith

258

When I was heterosexual

Books obeyed me

It says in *The Road Less Travelled*

With the water waiting far off

Book signing to which nobody came

The petit-bourgeois small shopkeeper hugs her small children
& kisses their heads

Heady & reckless smoke damaged smoke upon her breasts
smoke

The smoke from Mothercare going up love & the sirens I
am—

(A)

Text

Mother

Loaded with E.L.O. albums

Hiding in the bushes

Insanely happy & in love with life

259

Wobbling with emotion

In Worcestershire lonely as a newsagents & perpetual

Satiated by a pre-pubescent reading of Marx   his shadow

To run away from everybody with a moustache   sighing

For a world of women when there are none

It is impossible to resolve the issues of nationality with sex
doctor

For when I asked her she would not take the magic pills

& it is still physically impossible to engage in the story or to
have it

Timing is something that eludes both the stars and us

We bang our heads together over wanting it

When I wander all night in my vision (& I do)   Thomas—

Our critical mass

Consists mainly of gas

But then—these days—Who is "we"?   What is "us"?

260

When the sea leaves a fish   it stops being a fish

In the same way that it's only possible to have knowledge of
a body

Or of god upon earth fracking for jihad

Instead of all stars no star of which

ever waits

ten minutes

Unlike all the other high celestial and immortal forms

Imagined then sanctioned by the higher beings

spent in advertising

What is the point of a life's work of gags?

The longer the writer stares at poems   dogs   suns

The eyes reach out

& attempt to find meaning

The less they seez it

261

The aim of literature…is the creation of a strange object covered with fur which breaks your heart.

Donald Barthelme

Listen—

My woman loves to beat people

Never says I love you   loves cakes & rice instead

Her thighs are like reams of wrapped up newspaper ready for
    recycling

She kicks a man out of bed

Uses petrol to bleach her skin

If a dog is a real dog then like a dog she'll marry

Not for his money   just the feel of him

& if the plague swells your face it is good to hear her
    laughing

She crushes children that go fart & sing

My woman cries before no man except little animals

If I hunch down on all fours

One day if I am good

Will she see me   like them

262 for Koto

You fell from an ovary in the night
& entered my leg   shining
When I least expected it
Love with desire is not true love because
Stemming from emptiness it requires fulfillment thus
You saved me when I was scraping my face
& you saved me in Horace in Somers Town when
My ego grew huge famous &   (how)   stupid
With the thought of contentment
As I toss you towards this planet's twin suns   with your new
        shoes on
I think of death & how the turds fell like rain
On life twice   you know nothing about how I suffered
        with a surfeit of love
Koto   I you & we
From one golden ovary
Rise high in flight   always   shining & free

263

Because in the mind all is perfect

& there is little salt

Because it passes like a cake

A little counseling is enough

& as for   we who love to be abused

On water or on fire may   taste & good touch

Because there is no mind   because

Because the majority of cave dwellers are dexterous with
        pens

Because they fit

Because yuppies always move south

Because it is easy to blame the green vegetables

Because a single thought is always too much

Because burning is of use to describe humans

Put it out

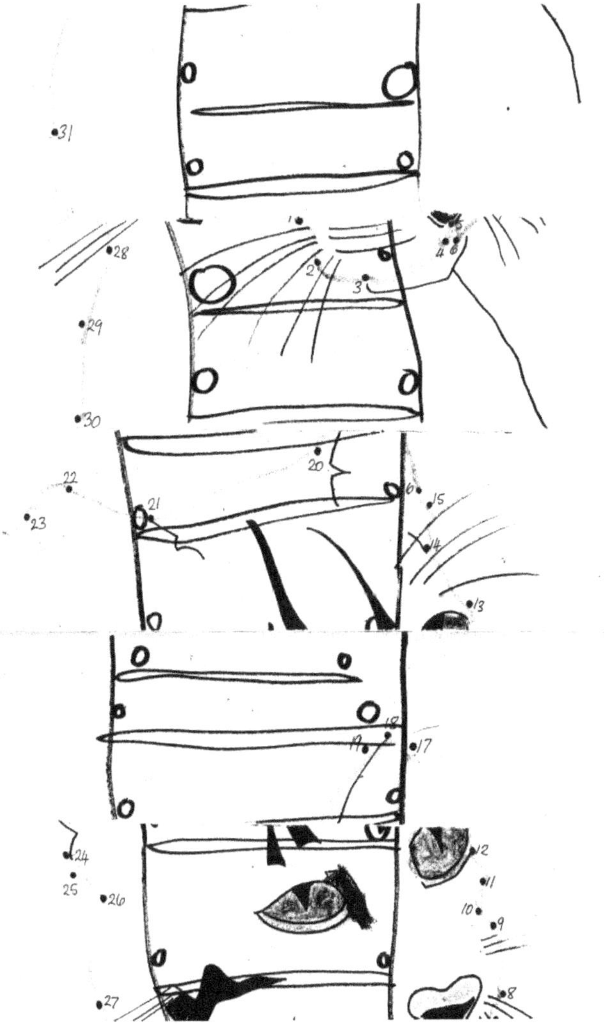
31
1
28
2
5
4
6
3
29
30
20
22
16
15
21
23
14
13
18
19
17
24
12
25
26
11
10
9
27
8

264

I go thinking & this thinking

Fills me with such

That I often find myself

At the end of it

Desperate for completely different reasons

Which is   that the end of life comes

& all the times I've asked the yoga 12-step or spiritual
practice shelf

On beanbags & in diners

When you should be looking at the page or the desk

Nail and shape which you fall for

Leaf crumb bending & black eyebrow

Book award competition

Attachment which jams you up to this fading   1962
incarnation

In which you can neither breathe nor leave

Rolling down the New King's Road in the dust

Lust winking the filth out for a second then banging it back
in

The answer as you know in every machine is within

As long as the sun rises on anything

Smeared with Tiger Balm & newsprint

One April night—coming

Like a big foot coming   then for an eternity   & its
    relentlessness

Down on love everything

In print   & the hope of small press

For what?   Something lasting like a language   which dies as
    it lives

Like a fabulous roman candle—& then sad in Jack Kerouac

Incandescent for several minutes

& hereafter   bad tempered & drunk   the language I suppose
    you know   dies with me

Really

At least if I go beyond

Thinking I would

Like this   go free

Like an aspirin

With the line up the middle   smooth

& round like Pythagoras' magic number

Or ball & chain in J. Joplin & S. James

Invisible to any gods

Jumping up & down   or ridiculous

In what remains of the night

Everybody knows that love is nowhere

When the icecaps are melting

& I walk past the hotel video capsule in which it is still
        possible

To draw the curtains & believe that she believes herself   too

Eternally beautiful & to look at this wound

like any famous fucked-up lovers or ex-boxers

Eventually shrivelled videoed & hairless

Walking the strip malls of Osaka

Pink & blinking—sticking it in

Before 10 million miles of real or imaginary cold men or cold
        women

In these poems

What need is there ever to write of anything

Other than love and the prospect of fucks

If all weaklings are honest   it's beaver Las Vegas or bust

Equality & communism

Or for lack of it come

Fucked at the start of a good life means many things

By the end it means one

All the new rules that I've recently made concerning organic
food & meditation

Turn to ashes when I read Apollinaire think & go thinking

Without end finally on the green slopes

Of her breasts

This and the rest

Is just noise

Because god

Fries all men like

Little chickens

& the old poems

Vanity press

Everyone dies before you die

Let me prove it

Laura—

These

words

are

just

tests

265

It is the same thing forever & I am
Attempting to bring her round
Through all the tricks which did not work
When used on the ailing London Underground
Wanting her back more than The Beatles
Days spent at the pubic ranch
Who buys a hand swept across the forehead
Poem which couldn't put the legs back on a child whose legs have been blown off by a landmine
Though they may save a living man
In a soap wash Laura
All the things I ever wanted from you (dead) may yet come true
I need them to
At the great poetry revival
In which we came second

266

& once I wrote 15 haiku   in a day

On my back beneath a hedge on the Malvern Hills

& the fawns & small rabbits licked every bump of my body
    then

Before I had hair   & which now grows abundant off   my
    every ledge & shelf

It is 18 years in this poem   of combing

It one way this & then the absurdity   next

Of any 14th century male addressing himself to

A woman or god   —both ideas of which went down in
    flames in the late

19th Century according to Nietzsche or Henry James—

Made worse by the invention of hair gel

Sticking itself down in the wind   & yet

My balls are still big in this

Hurricane if they can't break

Friedrich at least   let them bend

267

21 years of tandoori can save no-one it seems

neither Laura nor me   from the back of the car seat   on fire
or the

cells that fall off the ends of the fingernails

bad other parts   which are also in flames   & the wars
perpetuated

by those who call themselves lovers   standing in front of
their families   all in flames

without & who are burning too & the gas from fracking fills
the lungs & can never be breathed back out

& the words that go down are evidence of this & when they
are gone their small ash will say

enough perhaps in the eye of whoever steps in it having
hoped

like me to be received by the world instead of indifference
all

bills & trips which rip me regularly right out of my mind

flaming blown out by these winds   hear me now   Love   &
henceforth desist

year after year of Grand Nationals & the horses who go
down

& the Pandas & River Dolphins who just give up

beasts who once lived & no longer

268 for Stacy Doris

In *The Frozen Planet*

I do not think of penguins

Gathering to protect their young

Toss Frisbee or measure the length of Golden Gate Park

By stretching

But in it

Where once

I was an apartment in Manhattan

& you too & this husband

& the star points in yr ovaries had not yet descended too

Becoming children

Who are here now

Who is ever really

Here now as long as they'd like

Stacy

In the way that they'd like it

269

& no living writer can join her
Walking up & down Oxford Street
& if you look at me too   I am how
Music died in (you name the date)
Geezers in capes
Have wrecked our ship & this language
You can close both my eyes now
& blow out the candles
Like a love of the east
& the crushing of modernism
Touching knees to symbolize romance
In a scene otherwise lacking
Proclaiming the triumph of compassion
Acting = reality if you believe in it too
As perhaps still she sees me
Just in case
the heart is most broken by joy
& with a crack happens out of itself
only on the most polluted of days

ozone or high pollen count

You split the details of her eyebrow

Silence & big leg so often that there is

I am waving this hankie

She is dead now really dead so

Not like in books

Where the dead are

But in life where the dead aren't

Except for Walt Disney

270

That there are other women & I go forward
Thinking of their pine larch or rosewood
& I think of the pale skin which covers their wrists
Moving over the evening
& I think of many women—bad or good
Leaning back in a ladder-backed chair
& I think of a low dress
& then my beard comes back
& she of these sonnets
Beyond the sea of G
& no longer forms
Who never said anything except about food to me
Whose horoscope was always right
Who used her left hand
Who had 26 moles
Spat as hypertext
& avoiding bright sunlight & children
Whose legs entertaining in church touch with money
Disappears

For the nature of life is

Pressing hard on my pencil

Because it fills up the sump

Under the trees in autumn

Of all woman & want

You who like it

Because everything is half dead

& that is the good half

Left here

In a large automobile

Or cassette tapes

& still life

With lumberjacks

271

I am a man made of pale blue plastic & since I have fallen
over am

Frequently on the receiving end of Keats's negative
capability being empty

& wanting to be dead never happened because of tequila

& I am on my side & there is dust on my right

& it is impossible to move

"illumined" in the shadows of alleys "by burned-down
candles,

dripping and smoking"

sexless in the world because then they can't sell it

smelling good beside a lake mooning eating again mooing

a woman & the popular science books' descriptions of stars

know that filaments eventually burn everyone out

the need to mourn the passing world's turns

like the lonely clowns beating their drums on empty streets

in the late lithographs of Daumier or Baudelaire's "pitiful"
acrobats

272

Adorno's famous saying, it seems, needs correction: it is not poetry that is impossible after Auschwitz, but rather prose.

Slavoj Zizek

Is there a President anywhere of anything

Smoking can affect

A soldier speaking into the camera saying "when we had him
we had him"

The long withdrawal of television

Cups all over the body

Sleep means you do not love the world

We get the pigs & we skin 'em

Vomiting

In search of Hart Crane

The spirits of the soldiers disappear across the fields

This computer will give you ten years of life &/or love

Issa is

That star with the long number which I saw last night when I
went out

Just went out

273

Recently returned from parts unknown

Scrubbed & oiled like a seven-piece boy band sagging on a
 bed

The heart rolls in out of habit attachment

Forms crusts over the author

Elephant or invisible man

There is this cartoon book bible & in it god makes a good
 man & drops him

& he comes down & he sings till he's dead

We Are The World & I think WE are the world

Pursued by her single black eyebrow

On John Clare's grave—A Poet is Born not Made

The Men by Lisa Robertson & Imagine

A poet is born not mad

What you thought

He said

274

They take the prisoners & dress them in

Fashionable orange

They make the mustard gas

Incandescent yellow

They paint their faces to appear spooky or serene

They take the prisoners   undress them   & then

They get off

Pointing their bombs towards oil or towards Allah   is that

Not enough?

In the sticks it is half

War all the time

The dog   chews my leg

When I stay late in bed

We have no one to blame but ourselves

275

& so   I   once more   want to see her with my mouth
& would press my eyes on her small & large sounds
& apply my ankle to her coldest parts
I would hold her small car until it breaks
Place my pencil alongside her
Shred her clothes & then mine & then live in them
Gather all the air from the dead room to swim in
& grow breasts of gold the better to know her
I would feel sexual for Johann Sebastian Bach in South
        Kensington
Discard every feeling which made me ever human
To go on through the centuries singing—
Eat every colour which touched her
In order to end it   once and for all
Unscrew my bad parts   & leave them

276

If the meaning of love is to fuck forever

Then this

Instead of writing

"this is how etc."

& in love with it

is keeping it

From slipping off the page   a woman

Forever dropping through the real world

& against this

Page

Bad Honey

I Rage

In the "knock, knock" joke concerning Death

You never get to the end of

276.2

How boring to be bored with being bored with love

From any interest aroused in the amorous subject by the
    loved body

Yuk— You get up & return to Adorno

The postcards of Che & of Liam glued to a quote in place
    of a heavenly altar

Karma (the machinery, the classroom) functions in front of
    me but without

Clouds have not been mentioned but to be a cloud would be

Projected onto the other with such power that when I am
    without the other I cannot

Etymology the eyes corners

An ant on the margin is not the same as the joys of a baby

From the top of tall buildings

A lover looks down on all sentient beings

& Flies for all that as a cloud

Sees in small wings

The sadness in things

277

When my hair was long and black

Reading *Hammer of the Gods* with Miles Champion in
    Camden

& *Spring In This World of Poor Mutts*

How happily we bandied our mullets

When my fingers all worked & the art school at Dartington

Dangling theory over words

It's impossible not to love from a position of excess

Although now I do daily meditation   ennui

Organic gardening   & tai chi—

Having abandoned sex   love   beauty   martini

The truth is

No   friends—they—

All five (four, or three)

Abandoned me

278

Dead exactly 3 years

& for 3 long years dated 6 April 1351 without rice or ramen

She—who was & is

No longer incandescent with jealousy   or childless over
    children

Burdened by even less human feeling than when living

Now long dead must be—if the dead can make love then

Perhaps we have more chance than on earth us both living

In a house to be dead in   if the living can find them

Needless of books body warmth or   human shopping

With an etch-a-sketch condom

Of this author's imagination his great love

Un-invented & unavailable for dating   only here

In this poem is her floating dead body

Warm only   in the author space   living

Cold   beyond Italian even all human feeling

Never wrong for the dead never can be

Heart frozen since the moon landing

Here is to say I love you in a vacuum

But still saying it dead or alive still

Hope & keeping that feeling

279

She who I—

Bland with defending the avant-garde establishment

Rainfalls on her dead heart   & coming off hard   or

Hits on my own   & the steam rising   Laura—

Incredible   with the speed of the red shift   from infatuation
to death

Blind in the face of the   void   of   needing as much

Testosterone to lift the skin off & place a roof on it

Horizontal in a field   & hope   for the stars' sparkler dins to
stick in

Here   sexless & full   as a skyscraper

In the neon sky   leaving a line

Blue-pink   black   or   cracked

A lover who comes upon a lover

Without a sexual bone in her body

Least of all mine

280

Sitting upright in front of a lie detector

A male nurse devoted to a woman called Pam

Coming in with a dose of Phil Spector   & failing test after
test

Like the pot test and the one involving fire and domestic
dwellings

& the proof of seriousness   test   which is essential

In order to discover any new planet

In a prose poem entitled "The Shrimp Exaggerated"

There is a rare tulip in the middle of this soil & we   am
that tulip

My name is Jean (pronounced Gene)

In London SW19

The camera records everything but love

& on the other hand   again   Love

If you can get it from my kung-fu grip

Then you can have it

281

Boiling in summer

Freezing in winter

Obsessed with the tiny flecks of paper from bottle tops &
necks which cover my nest

Fraught   like sunlight

Sticking into my back & tongue

Finding love   when in disgrace

Except in this

Feminine

Syntax & content

On high days & holidays

A whole school of poetry

Knowing nothing of anything women

& this one—not!

Whistling   if not singing

282

In the

What-is-Bo Diddley's-hair-like-underneath-his-hat

Koan

Men in Aida

Know or have known

The impossible yoga

& life itself

a political question

Upon the Carrer d'En Robador—in Barcelona

Every choice that you made was

A rum one

Yet among cats it is always

Fear & sorrow

Laughter & weeping

283

To get here without having come

Some men blame others & others blame death

But wherever I look or step

I think of the day that I was the new king of hip-hop

Doing lines at a desk

& I think of Popeye   & the Plays of the Noh

& then I remember the shape of your word in my ear which
        was

But one ear & one word

How that lasts

& even how   to inflame the hearts   of tigers & bears

I wanted to do good things with women or wood

On Bear's Head

But all now that's left's

The memory of Spain in my chest

284

Here I stand on a bridge in Avignon

        In my wedding dress

Like a woman in love

        Who has just stepped off

A motorcycle

        In the dusk in September

& the dust is upon my young legs

        & my throat is a brilliant white-

Black and the swallows

        Reflected upon the water

Longing for cigarettes

        As soft as my woman's armpits

Or cool-warm stone is

        Cool-beautiful from looking

& over the mountain

        Where it is night

Plums appear in the poem

        & then sleep

As the body floats

Out of the body

Towards Barcelona

In the mind of all spiders

I like to beat people up

Vs. I Love You

For the sonnet is not dead

When is a cough not just a cough?

Somewhere over the rainbow

R.S.I. / rsvp

285

When the dead speak

The radio Mondays

Work to make women equal to men

Vitamins determine the natures of houses

Calling like a bird calls another bird

& fights for it

When there is too much evidence of love in the concrete

It is necessary to go to the poem & erase all the bum notes

Reference to livers or legs   & then

A man shuffles from memory to experience & back again

Heaven I wished for vs. heaven received

Defeat snatched from the jaws of victory

Is it possible to be both happy and in trouble

Robert Browning bending over the body Elizabeth Barrett
Browning

286

When I think of myself

as a woman

Careful when handling chilli

& do not speak

In a haiku like this

Men enter with text

It says & goes backwards forever

In polemical books (all—

Predictive with dread

It was possible to feel it

In Camberwell

Laura the dead cannot see how

The dead speak

Because they are not dead

287

When the dead speak

& you speak back to them Tim

In the middle of a rash sobriety & incandescence

Because the mountains would not

come to me

I will

go to

them

& live

there forever yeah

sore

soar

over

everything

288

No blackbird's rung upon which I climb

Its echo   the whole day

Homeopathic stars

Kindle L & her

Elbows in tune

Upturned towards the

Skies of Worcester

Spent in a book ward

In a book note at England

In August forever

Remembered but

Not for me

Here & there & then

With pen & paint & pains

289

& I am dreaming at my workstation in tall buildings working

on a pie chart & bar chart

concerning the beautiful flow of cash in & cash out & the
cloudlight

on the gleaming buildings cerise slice of pie representing
29% of the notion of growth & the unacknowledged
legislators of mankind

beside the pale orange piece which stands for 63% of
information light

the cursor's shadow as it crosses the screen & mouse also
beautiful

cool in the cupped palm of my hand

comfortable as the small of my back which is a joy forever

rests against the convex black leather of the ergonomic office
chair

& swivels to face the bin into which my left hand throws a
crumpled sheet of

pleasingly white paper & upon which I once wrote this & my
eyelids

twitch &

the table is just unemployed coffee you are still dead there are
no poems writ really & there is now only me (sic)

I begin to waken & see

290

Ulysses knew women & the art of lying

More so for those in love

Venice suggests itself

Ravaged by seating

How the world changes

So much so   hopping not hoping

As sad as a nose   the world its & I am

For Mario & Luigi

It is war all the time &

The bright obvious stands motionless in the cold

With or without

Her

Good

Plumbing

291

It is growing lighter in London

The little birds & their fast hearts move up from the ring-
 roads & stop

Arrested by the lights of 7Up & the dark off the common

Making their way in the world with small vehicles

& those in their nests warm themselves by flat-screen light &

Incandescent for the one who carried my thoughts off with
 her still

There is snow on the cracks which highlight my lack

The clock's on yesterday & the angry birds call themselves
 then

Those that break say that I am awake

I don't believe you when you say (but you do) that you

Prefer more handsome men &

Less passionate birds—

Love—

Perhaps it lies to you too

292

My eyes which are good green eyes & which go
Arms which are short arms
On the mother's side most hairless
Touching the eyelids to find the love point
The nameless orange set
Which is "an obligation to share" met by chance & by force
The G spot being where a man planted his flag
After 15 years in a village of imagination & boredom the night or the day is
Dry in the vein of habitual art
Dull as in over & Dull as in lightless
& Then it comes yet again (trouble)
The waft of a woman
Political incorrectness
From over the fence

293

Life is the meaning of life

But gets in the way of it

Klee said I am taking the pencil for a walk & I am saying
yes to everything

As a counter to Love's value's depreciation the rising of

Resentment & oblation which I aim to

Surmount without liquidating for what I

Have affirmed a first time in April I can

Affirm again for what I affirm is the affirmation

I say to the other old or new silent weary & still—

After her Ahoy! Bonjour! Is anybody listening?

Let us begin again

Life is the meaning of life

But gets in the way of it

I desire its return not its repetition

294 (these lines to be read in any order)

Alive I would have kissed her neck

in any foreign field

with the sea stretching out from my feet

like love we often keep

lovely dark & deep

& thick on Severn snow

the turbid ebb & flow

within my inmost soul

never beams without bringing me dreams

hung aloft the night

but hope is just

shadow & dust

you fail or pass

& then you go bust

295

I

kiss

you

in

the

nursery

behind

the

screens

in

your

grey

house-

coat

10th November 1864—to his wife

296

Concerning the beauty of the world & the things living in it

Autumn appears beneath the tattoo

& the husband =

A cure for airsickness which

rises   because   everything real is first imagined

in the eyehole   its finger points towards the door

dreaming of freedom & the immortality

hanging beyond love & its affectations

like the new age we were promised in the 1960s

free like free milk is   & then again

the cogs wear down

beside all rumor & politics

forever caught in it

at the base of the modernist

297

& chemotherapy removes all trace
Of Wordsworth & the romantics   from the lesson
Which is to see as opposed to annotate or amputate   every
    leg   as it emerges from the body
Which I am guilty of
Approximations of her   digital life
Instead of having the chance for consecration
In the company of others entitled   either or before   the
    beauty of the word
Which constitutes her name spelled thus
By the romantically approximate
Swooning on the omnibus towards Clapham
As lovers do
As beautiful as an ant   its gracious acts   the wise and
    humble speech
Employed   only & often
So as not to be forgotten

298

Years of amazement staring at her back

& the years spent in theme parks

Longing for her front

Years spend staring into the city wasted in tubes

Years spent writing letters concerning the possibility of work

Years among acts of more-or-less charity

In various states of punctuation

Years spent avoiding

Years spent listening to how to listen & then how to say it & then

Life as a flipping burger flipper or artist of unrecognized genius for eternity in a helicopter

Hovering over & above love's dark thing

4 decades coughing

An existence without ever ironing a shirt properly

My longing to change it

299

In this poem is the beauty of the husband diminished

By years of solar   stellar   &/or (reflected) lunar light

The voice that mourns the coming death   of instinct   and
        rails   against the coldness & narrative arc of
        masculine hegemony & homogeneity

In a hotter & scarier world   hence this author   Tics   for
        fear bad faith & lack of meditation

The dead father appears & says   nothing

The best advice I ever had came from the horoscope page
        (Leo) of *The Daily Mail* (which said)

& where is the noble shadow of that face that refreshed my
        weary soul & the place where I wrote it

Where also is Khaled Hakim   his rewritten English   noble
        shadow & written permission?

Once more   silence

Where in this instance

Also Sprach Tim Atkins

& just

Outside   my   mouth

Her fiery biscuits

300

Puddly concupiscence of the flesh &
The hot imagination
Turns the pages listlessly
Of a book about
The Angry Brigade
Love once more
On a cold day in spring
The pale moon
Rises upon
My white hump
Departing from Argos
I do not look
Like a soldier at all
I look like a filthy flamingo

301

I call on Death to help me combat Death

With such dark thoughts Love fills my body's weight

& the woofing of dogs will not save me & the light which
saves and protects—

Visions of the sexual imperative instead of the fits of dawn

Beneath the beautiful blue buildings

& the smell of sex in the hair of all Italian boys & girls

In the same way that beauty is untenable & utopia is
unfashionable

On the beach where Shelley's black heart would not burn

The sky is full of marbles & my mouth

Subjective in cafes whilst reading

The chains of the objectivists the Laika poem   & the
milkshake   the matchboxes & the stamps of space

Inhabiting the gaps when the knees open

The cats all walk out when I attempt to talk of her   dance or
play

Purple Rain

302

If the sonnet is a room   which is a room
For all life to perform in—
Then it is preferable to have one with a window desk & toilet
At which to sit in (& this is it)—&
Then they say that death is like
Taking a tight pair of shoes off
For three years in Spain
Pointing my toes at the swallows
In the blue Catalan sky
I was in love with more than just food
It is not true
Here   with you   for almost a fortnight
For one limitless instant
I remained   almost   in heaven

303

Unfaithful to the idea of love because it does not work

How you want it to

Unlike a sea-horse

Like a language does

Through the colour of mood ring urine sample or aura—

Consigned to a nick-nack nook

When you have something worthwhile to say about
Wordsworth

The criminal presidents & prime ministers

Their books & their mansions brogues napalm & landmine
collections

Burping into jars eating wasabi chicken wings

Reading *Fifty Shades of Grey*—writing *Fifty Shades of Beige*

Speaking out against fur at the conference

Meaning it shaking & the need

To turn it all off

304

Here I am at every a.m. incomplete

The air is on the far side on the way to normal

I drink some poofter's froth and am inanimate

The streets of London look as lovely as a woman from Japan

I run around caressing them

Who would have thought that I'd be here?

Not good old me or the bookshops of the Charing Cross Road
        or the boring long & windswept stretch of the Strand

Had or even dad

The tinnitus says Frank

My poet thoughts go through my head: ____________

I am occasionally successful in attaining my aim of No
        Thought

When will I sink?

Alone and untenable   I slip softly upon *The Dolch Stanzas*
        listening to punk

The world's glorious song flows through my sarong

305

in kanazawa
mid-august
the crickets
metal jackets
fine light
hits the
iris like
gray tears
through an
old kimono
no knees
so sore
the buddha
cannot cure

306 for & from Jackson

them eyes & the forehead

of 1 plant honour

which celeste I do not novo

the sky gets lost

with the eyes bathing the grass and the chest

but returning me to mind

pon breaking

I recognize in you the used ones

meco et with the river

that me it made

In other part it does not spur to me

distant & sleeping

shadows caves waves

to me double the evening

307

On the 12 streets of Soho   where the light hits the eyes

Gangsters still need the vanity of a little sunshine

& The Movement   sucking on or   tanned perhaps

In a syrup   a series of growls   or complaints about living
        look

If you want to learn about the world   he said

Bob Creeley & Zuk really!—even Walt—making things up

Suddenly   exasperated   shirtless   hirsute & out of the
        country

Playing the bongos electricians do it all for you

The Emperor of China's elaborate chapbooks –

A ripple of piss

For the jaundiced eyeball   but

On the Costa del Crime

All life   (still)

Flares   through the pinhole

308

& so I exchanged air for helium   to breathe love for

To speak of it   squeaking

Day after day in a book by Madame Blavatsky   on a diet of

Cod stars & prediction   in an inn on Borough High Street
    & particularly   giving

My youthful life to the night sky

For what does it mean when you say   in the shadows of cool
    spring evenings

An eye fell out & rolled into love's best part

This is the love which was felt in my art

That particularly   which

Off my tits from spilling

I bite with my chalky valentine pencil

Sense of balance & lost

Act of   wondering

309

Being old is the book subject

Held together with bad sellotape

But for the ones with herpes   short ones   cleft palates

& Awaiting urn burial   in 67 sonnets

It is easy to be in love with the beautiful ones   singing with a
    good voice   towards & surrounding

Sucking in the cool blue air   smoke of a cigarette's smoke

Content for if the bad guys are asleep & silence surpasses

Everything in the Italian language

Often but not always enough   like koalas or elephants just to
    live as vegetarians

Without gender   looking at the moon like Nat King Cole

Pressing his bare feet into the cool grass of his Hollywood
    lawn

While the bad fucks keep grinding

The point of writing is to sing beyond what you know &
    remain   fast / awake

Love—This is the notion which feeds & informs me

310

The clocks go forward
& the flowers & the grass his sweet family
& Plant calls to page the weeping song
& springtime pure white pink blues
& laughing meadows & the sky rubs itself clean
It is always heaven to be with one's daughter
Air & Water & Earth abound with it
Each living thing turns towards love & is persuaded
But for me so far & always like the Worcestershire
Life is   agricultural & bassy   from my heart's crack
She sped towards heaven with the keys
& the singing of the small bjorks & fields in bloom
& women behaving in the air make this place
A desert & the beasts   still   harsh & savage

310.2

It was the golden age of homosexuality

Chairman Mao taking the buffaloes for a stroll in the tea-oil
    camellia groves by banana leaf-shaded ponds between
    Heathrow & Slough

Creatures of the sun-loving world   vs.   the pale less
    resistant ones

Avatars of insufficient definition or relation dressed in
    animal bird or cowboy forms

Head filled with poems until it was almost impossible not to
    trip over them   for example

Petrarch's shift between need to write   fame   and singular
    woman

Alas! My Place Is

With

This   Fuck in this life

Surprise is all I have

I never learned

To turn quickly enough from

All that burns

Feeling each other up and liking each other terrifically all the
    way home from the Odeon

310.4 for & from Surrey & Drew Gardner

The soft bosom that bit me and bloke fur binges
With gene bath clad the balti and shag the vole
The nightingale with reefers how she sings
The turtle to fist graphic formalism for tools
Sorrow to come and queer quotes and new strings
The last bath thong his hot pole with salt
The lymph in the bottle his wit in part springs
The lobes deep with mold's repeated sales
The whites all but buggered above the swingers
The swift elbow pasturizes the shemales
Their balmy forays to mince with the mingers
Witless to hymen that was the famous tale
As I go smogless among pleasant syringes
The ravers decay yet my spray tan still stings

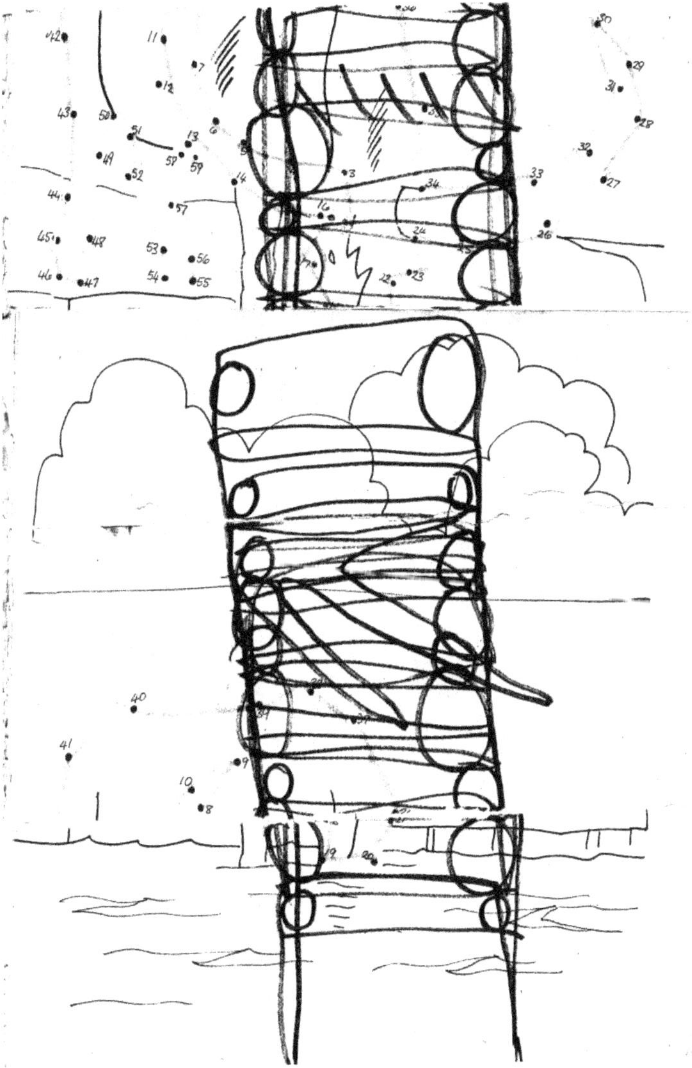

311

Life spent in a potting shed listening for diamonds

Staring into the night sky   at the bottom of the table of
elements

With a cloud book for companion

It is easy to be reminded of the darkness of the earth

Where love clings & the living cannot penetrate

I have wasted my life downloading

The salts from my head without heeding the needier organs

In the middle of the night we go   plip plop   plip plop

In the Writer's Handbook in Tooting

My love for her raised absentmindedness to an art

& wiped the slate clean of all human feelings

As other voices fill the sky   below Betelgeuse I notice

The cockroaches running between my toes

Until   finally   I begin writing

312

No lovely small noisy birds with dark shiny feathers that
roam through empty pieces of clothing for a woman or
girl that hangs from the waist

No well-oiled water creature with a shell upon a tranquil
person who does sculpture

No place where old or injured horses are taken to be killed
and their flesh sold in low comfortable chairs with
supports for the arms through the part of a cheque
ticket etc which can be detached and kept as a record

No swift and frisky tall thin people in charming women
especially the women of a family or community
considered together

No recent tiny piece of atomic matter of long-awaited thin
sticks covered with a substance that burns slowly and
produces a sweet smell

No small piece of material sewn into a garment of a small
insect living on the bodies of people or animals in lofty
ornate state of being nearly unconscious or not fully
aware of what is happening

Nor there amid clear small young onions and red hats with a
flat top and tassel but no brim of green

Sweet device or system for finding objects under water of the
production of milk by women or female animals
virtuous and lovely

Nor other part of the human leg between the knee & the hip
can ever touch my number of things or mass of
material lying in an untidy pile

She buried it so deep with her own instrument for detecting
earthquakes

Who was alone for my extreme views in politics or religion a
person employed at a beach or pool to rescue people
and a girl who is playful or cunning and does not show
the proper respect

So long and heavy is the pain of animals kept on a farm for
use or profit

That I call for the books giving information about every
branch of knowledge so much I want

To see the official appointed by government to investigate
and report on complaints made by citizens against
public authorities I should never have seen

313

Gone is the time
                    Endlessly required to define the
When I was pleased by the rules of love's games
        loved object like
Pen &c gone for whom I
        A merely liberal who no longer "sticks" exonerated
Consign to the flames
                    From every adjective
Thus (gone) the (lost) tube top
                    thus and no other
Bus pass & safe houses to steam in
        experienced
Or skip over the cracks
                    As a heavy invertebrate with an appetite for
        surprise
A pint of milk or to follow her
                    Experienced as a cowardly stubbornness
Underground & then up
                    In the realm of amorous sentiment
Wherever the light combs
        This is the world of replacement

Avoid a man tantrums
Or again

For want of butter
who can leave without his

That holds me here by force without credit
image

Sighs like the blessed souls calling me
crumbling?

313.2 for & from bill bissett—with love

gone is the time when I played happily in the fire

gone is the time when I thought of her and these words

gone is the girl who pierced these parts with longing

gone is my heart which failed only to follow her

gone coz she took it down when she died to the sky

gone thus as a prisoner in my own body

gone beyond the out breath

gone shining new among the souls uv the blessed

gone

gone

gone

gone

gone

nd the leaf uv the heart is shining

314

Oh my mind which foresaw all this

loss worried & sad morbid even in happy times

sought to store up some succor for future troubles this her

ankle again words boats or dogs

fish attempts at drawing circles

waters lousy parking habits avoidance

of runner beans infatuation with

borderline sense of direction sparkplugs

management skills neckline & hands

black from working the soil attraction to

composting meat of the whale logic for safe keeping leave in
her

beside my heart   now this

weak art

my softest part

314.2

I went to parenting classes   toneless   like babies   & broken
    in triplicate

To get away from my kids

Now I take polaroids of skies

Rubbing their little hands together

Ruined by dogs poems such as this

Until the manufacturers refuse to make paper

Wife to miss [or love] (line 1)

Bamboo grass put on [or to dive under] (line 2)

………(line 3) (several words missing)

Floating like a brown paper bag over Tooting

When a fly treads too heavily on the carpet

I went to obedience training

& it was going well till they spilled wax on my private parts

Look—here is my certificate

315

Before there were thickening agents

There was language

Before there was language

There were waters

Made from off-cuts of Flavor Flav and Gary Numan

The nothingness of our beginning is hard at work to bury us

I belong to structuralism and to skiffle—

With its affectations and haircuts   bi-polar moments

Conspicuous consumerism & Iliassa Sequin

The last time the Tories noticed you

You were their cleaner

The last time the Republicans cared about you

You were a fetus

How none of you can ever really know me

316

The oral life (first here) in the lovely young sex books
& tent light

(I said here second) boings back up against the strong
nuclear force

For this is (here below) the 21st century & I am inside it
(that is not to say)

(I do not go on saying) in a car in the country outside
Oxford & (all there) it still be cigarettes

& fossil fuels even taste (I do not go on saying)

(that is not to say) good in the mouth sucking the thing
directly in front & holding it as if like to lovers

(here) beside one man's heart (there) rolling out
understands me (here and there)

& from which (I do not talk first) (say there) they told me

She was no longer Leon Trotsky in a garage band this
cardboard prose as different from my dark &
mellifluous line

As is possible on this earth friends (here below) (under my
words) (I do not talk down) (Here and there)

Thought I was someone (Here below) but was not living

(Here below) (Here and there) (Here and there)

The Gay Life (I do not say it now) meaning in men

In a happy state

316.2

Filled with the anxiety of influence

& with P.G. Wodehouse   in Spring—is that your answer to everything?

Pronouncements concerning the fact that we will be happy only when everybody in the world is proclaimed as a poet

Having a nightmare either in or about the Bario Xino in Barcelona

Demanding that the cocktails answer back

I did not know how much I did not know about Joan Miró

Sitting on the lap of a woman or a man & admiring their earlobes

The ones Eric called "niggers"

You click the text box for Japanese Greetings & select one for August

貴社ますますご盛栄のこととお慶び申し上げます。

How good it is to be baffled by language and

How good it is to be small & inconsistent

Now that not only does the beloved's body disobey the author's inclinations & orders

But so does the author's

317

An egg rolls down & then out of   A woman

One which you wanted   but could not catch

You ponder the origin of wool

Then a little more food with holes in

Flat on the bed from boring   grey-eyed and moated as if in a
    moat

Words in freedom some of them reunite to make The Art
    Ensemble of Chic

A woman   with rope & a bad magic trick

Skipping like   the record does in order to caress into being a
    new age of feeling & that which is lacking

As you pour yourself a small cup of humanism this is it—

Your life work sky or author function resting in the body

Which you both admire & revile   in one stocking believing
    once more

As the teeth fall in to love   you could   however—

In spite of all dental & medical evidence

Leave them there forever

318

The increased airport capacity which spurs me on

To further heights of insolvency

High on the DLR above the light receptacles bankers &
burgers

A flat stomach & surrealists for eternity

Like sex with I wrote for on a white floor with the
splinters puncturing my or your upside-down body

As he enters me

I mean you

Dead seriously

Only then will you come—

So badly & So much

Dreaming of the beautiful men & women

On the fronts of seed packets

Ox-eye daisies & the purple ones

Begonias & nasturtiums

318.2

Because bad credit means suffering

By which I mean   massive & blunt   makes me

Wandering—How long have I been wandering

As bequeter means to peck or to pick up crumbs

Tracking a teardrop for a comma into life's vast promise

Always the same—

The struggle of Mind   to reach The Thing

Which for lazy men is impossible

Burned by fur

Eating chips in the rain

Conquered by custom & almost ceasing to function

With a shifting plume of radiation

Destroying the drawing-room furniture with a poker

All the way from Tooting Broadway

318.3

If the I is no longer meaningful & all that translation
makes me

For example (2) My Head Gets Tooken Apart in Hieronymus
Bosch's The Ascent Of The Blessed

Lined with (3) feminine regrets

Now let me list them

A position towards the loved subject or object

Passive-aggressive tendencies or part submission

In a world of exquisitely designed land mines

Where the sexual excretions of mammals clog the arteries

There is a little too much volume in the library & I am in it

I can see the letters where my love used to be on the page

Speaking from an enlightened position

If this is an out of the body experience I am having

& this is some kind of competition or test

My reply is this—Laura—I was never really in it

319

A man who writes for you

Because your arms don't work

Says I meditated myself out of my body

& woke up in Clapton

& my graphic novel

Walking before the beautiful sight of the tall buildings &
falling

My secret is

In the sense of love everybody

Lost in the big C which comes for me

The voices which enter the head

In the morning cereal promise

Whispers

Bomb in a whisper—then

Hairy toes & a new life with goats

320

When I read my old books about beekeeping
Before the materiality of the signifier crushed
The journals of Dorothy Wordsworth   Hair pie & cocktails
Which once were the breakfast of champions
The life of a flaneur lies heavy on the colon
&—in line 11—as they say—cold is the nest where I lay my breast
Good sense & younger men with felt-tipped pens
Have written it better because of the light & their beautiful forearms
It is Tuesday & I am become pumpless
"Freddo I'niddo" no less for a man with an aversion
To high heels on account of the height of women
Bent & bemoaning   their spectacular columns
Their efficiency at multitasking
Their problematic relations with (the pointlessness of) epics

320.2

& it is all very   & the nights in white satin (again) when
    there is   & who am I to say that

Because my leg never quite fit   the straight jar   stocking

& space travel with The Invisible Girl & beautiful in bedsits
    resisting

At last it is over & the sun is high upon old national buildings

& the bad paper contains a build-up of acid

For it is gay to be read by the eaters of tikkas & park goers

The poor dispossessed & lovers of poets

& the history of letters is still living

Nothing less   than everything   indicates the continuation of
    rimming

At last it is April Poland appears over the hill & the spring
    winds blow

The dandruff   from her   grave

One day my poems will say something of use to humanity

For now there is no point in missing

Anything & the pink cat ring

321

I won the Eurovision poetry prize in 1341

To perform for you with orange skin

Kicked by a donkey aged 42   & leaving my DNA on him

Officially the world's first tourist

Eating calamari & cheap cigs

Feeling European in Europe

Al fresco   which means slightly aroused

By the warm hair

Smell of plane trees and train stations

Where I did love you with an earring

Sur la plage & then back at the hotel

A face full of crabs   instead of love

Is how great my love is

That is the question

322 for & from Naropa

Je Tim

When I dry your neck

I speak

Therefore

When I am someone's big toe

Then I am your whole

At the egg eating competition

Slathering mayonnaise round the grass

Your corneas like busted topaz

Your lips like lunettes de soleil

4 of them sticking out from a sunflower

3 eyes

Oracle oceanic eight   ocho-echo

& a tank full of sea monkeys

In ochre demise

Os—

T. Atkin & E. Sikelianoff

323 for & from Tom Raworth

1/ At the window

Under Tinicum or small Cohansey

Watching May become April again

Crossing the bridge of translation

With comics scissors & no overriding theory

Shoe philosophy or site of being alive

2/ & then at about ten thousand pages

In the bookmakers' art

Insatiable for concrete

Up to the earlids in babies

Wobbling is as wobbling does

At the protection of the cowslip society meeting

Being allergic to it

The smell of aircraft fuel on toast

Demanding breakfast for breakfast

3/ When ants arrived to give all 'the solution'

I built myself an ant box

If it is possible to love a city

This is my advertisement for a life

In a film called 'Blue Cowgirls'

In my apartment weeping

Over soft-focus pictures of puppies & kittens

4/ A man attracted to nylon

Perhaps should not go into space

In the Jardim Botanico or his molecules singing

This world of land mines & discarded legs & more landmines

All things rust to their end I wrote rushing

At midnight the slim male body enters the summer lake

Holding the book at arm's length the better to know it

What I loved most—frozen daiquiris   electricity pylons
typing

5/ How many lights are there yet to come on Daddy

For he is sleeping & you must climb up my back

Wearing a bearsuit to be warm in

6/ Across the lake of instant coffee

In a year in which they had cars

Having it in

I mumbled

About 6 quick trips

Then death's lips

As a poet   serious now & ambiguous

On stage at the Jack Kerouac School of Disembodied Poetics

Acting   beat & sexless   when really

I should have been ambitious

Denouncing all 23 of the things they don't tell you about
        capitalism

324 for Emily Critchley

What did she ever

know the beloved of

The dereliction of spiders or

The elbows of ants? What

do we as humans really

do on Lapetus?

Is there any beauty which

exceeds this?

How does the sonnet

approximate love?

Perhaps through this

*

Moon-

liness

325

Crayoned large enough to impress upon the world & the need
    to jump off it

at the edge of the eye where the cornea meets the A13

this hand is a wing and the other moving in front of the
    candle too thus painted

on the inside of Essex   is a bat or a bird

where music fears the ground of the stripmalls of Romford &
    Barking

& the light off the Cortinas & breast tops

touch the edges of the Thames Delta

in the detective novel   naked among warm summer leaves
    boys & goth girls

lovely to be fucking great for a while

lovely as patchouli oil on a woman called Lora from
    Birmingham

wearing white lipstick in markets & knowing the prices of the
    grapes & the melons

holding black orange pale blue & pink plastic products made
    in Hong Kong & not failing in conversation

reading Marx in the park & touching his cock

for all humanity beneath the shade of the trees

when we were French & were irresistible

when we wrote slogans about the necessity of roughage the
sexual imperative & blowing

when we were doing this men in polyester in the Caribbean

& men in polyester in the shitty peninsular states between
guessing & knowing

& men smarter than us in mixed fiber suits in lovely
buildings

going about their business kept on going

without our illuminating the insides of unmanageable
buildings

without sanction or knowledge fucking the destruction of
workers' collectives or non competitive contact sports

without loving the money behind which they lay hidden

barking worked   in the way that a dialect caresses a
language

& the tanks do not accept it

& the pixies & the fairies & elves then come in

& their little eyes rolling

& the confusion of police dogs

their shining fur

lovely for an instant

to both bite & be bitten

18 Alamo Road London SW19

finds all poets (-ah)   sleeping

in fear of the washing up rota

well sorted & thought   possibly

utopian & thoughtless   forever

surfing & outraged

in shoes narrow or broad   & therefore

immune from this system

hegemonic & bacterial

POETS! DUDES!

unconquerable therein snoring

Is this hell & are we in it?

326 for Musa McKim

as all your beauty took me down on earth

all your beauty took me down

as all your beauty took me

all your beauty took

all your beauty

as all your beauty took me down on earth

all your beauty took me

all your beauty too

as all you

all your beauty took me

as all your beauty took me down

all you

took me down

took me down on earth

327

& if a man can love a stretch of road

The one out of Worcestershire

Recommends itself to fair goers

Giving my love a goldfish

Trombone poem

Happenstance upon Herne Hill

I got the sack from the museum

For imitating a human being

My one mistake was

Choosing the wrong one

Watching the city in its final decline

Light from the flames

On my arms & legs

Dazzled by its magnificence

328

Mysticism is just a word. I am concerned with facts on all levels of experience.

William S. Burroughs

Friendly (in the Polish manner)
with Nat King Cole
sharing a cigarette with the kids
all day revising Petrarchs
to preclude love
I am sitting
on a blue chair
in a blue room
in my dreams
I experience a very nice example of verbal condensation
thin
king
of you
repairing the windows which the neighbors kicked in

328.2

& I fell into a burning ring of fire   & the flames   looked like
dirty snow

As one about to be assailed by tertian fever   is unable to feel
the raised digits of his card

& happy days   or press her cheek to the warm A4 paper

I said look at the stars to myself in the exit   & the raspberries

Like a premonition of death in the muscle bathed in the static
glow at the end of the video entitled cannibal zombies

Saying   Rimanetevi in pace (peace be with you friends) &
HERE late yet but not   (surely) fucked

She spoke in a glow these lines to me (deleted)   & I
stepped out of a burning ring of fire

I saw the salads rolling down the hill   & am   in the
ambulance

& the poet Horace recommends himself as a friend but I AM
him

His beautiful eyes now in heaven   with chaste strange
shining

Swimming in suburban delirium   unable to leave the house
without consulting the I-Ching   searching for magic
mushrooms but unsure

As in Lucretius   about the point of the tip & its effects on all
manner of speaking & then in poem 328

Shouting (3 times in this order)   the sonnet   the sonnets
the sonnet

Imperative—Interrogative—Affirmation

Innit?

329

& the O! Day & the hour & the O! stars in the horoscope &
the secret knowledge

In which she is more hidden from me than the hedge funds or
investment portfolios of O!

Those who speak to girls with tattoos & to people on trains

& who have knowledge of lichen & moss

Hidden from the waist down beneath the tables all longing

O! for a wind like in order to remove all doubt concerning
what it means to be human & in possession of all
human feelings

Like my little dog knows me & I inhabit him

For god fucks with fucks like us fucks in coffee table books

& we never thought of the invention of sclerosis in the liver
or wings

& the application & necessity of logarithms

Rising like breasts at 13 in us girls boys without knowledge
or abandon   poppers   & thai boxing

Standing in the doorway neither completely out nor in

Sorrowful & secret   autobiographical & overwhelmed
looking at the sky & the lightning   (like a lover)

Gone forever longing to be blown back blown over
or (ideally) Blown off

330

Here on earth & able to understand maps & smoke-signals

death is

my foot

most of all moves

everything that has been seen & will not go back

will have been seen

for nothing

or hands me

the mirror

& says

that's you

but does not tell me

what I am

no longer alive

no longer dead

I drift painfully

without existence & it will not go back

330.2

& Paul Blackburn who was dear to me   To whom I leave
these   writings

In order to translate me best   In Barcelona

Where I never was   As one who really sees it

& To get it all down   As one who imagined this
world

As it should have been   As it should have been

Holding the D   Above L

Because the alphabet   & Because a spider

Man light shines on the outside   I would not
allow

A Tim Atkins translation   As all men represent me

Being empty   & The Buddha fields

Upon which   Men being second

Serve each other   Stars as the air goes towards silence

With the fucks done   In capitals

Finally writing this   Self less & onward

331 for & from Lisa Jarnot

I used to sit at counters & admire anthropods & faux-
squirrels in museum light

In search of jerks of god following not free will but

Star coupons and often with cassettes of mostly harping
parping & squonking praying they would not

Jam bitterly feeding my heart As love does on magnesium
tablets cocoa solids

& voodoo powder

Now I—with hands up & left to fortune live like & yet
strangely not like a marsupial alone with its memories

My white tail rises though my soul is falling

It is perhaps the curse of the jogging classes to desire speed
over comfort & dolphin power

When neither clearly work any longer

The life of an artist consists of mooing more than mooing &
then cooing

Bipolar episodes / on buses

Side-stapled / perfect bound / selected then / collected

Crescent jerks

& then the endless

Mist & dust & holy water

WHY IS LENGUAGE IGNATZ ?
LANGUAGE IS THAT WE MAY UNDERSTAND ONE ANOTHER
IS THAT SO ?
YES THAT'S SO
CAN YOU UNDA-STEND A FINN OR A LEPLENDER OR A OSHKOSHER HUH ?
NO-
CAN A FINN OR A LEPLENDER OR A OSHKOSHER UNDA STEND YOU ?
NO
THEN, I WOULD SAY LENGUAGE IS THAT WE MAY MIS-UNDA-STEND EACH UDDA.

333

You are a hump or a sump grown massive through sleeping

On the bed of dread humanism

I am a mass of irritable French compound nouns

You clicking like a subject without form   but unlike a
racehorse

I am looking for a book entitled *50 Highland Wonks*   &
congratulatory fists

A louche & unreliable spider on holiday alone with
sandwiches beneath the Eiffel Tower

You no longer in The National Gallery the incandescent
clavicles of imagined & absent love jangling

Your cold fish diet gives out little   in or by northern
compass   & fridgelight

Planning upon my demise replacement with a honey-coloured
& emotionally horizontal asiatic tongue

"Taking out your gold teeth & delusions &"—like Harold
Robbins

"...placing them next to your opalescent literary non-literary
& dust-covered front"—like Jackie Collins

Too old to spot the difference

I am instead

A poet of somewhat perhaps eh?—Incroyable!

334

The job of the poet is to illuminate the   job of the poet
which is no job

Such as   My Confession   & collaged from   yon conceptual
canon

what it means refusing intercourse with the little what it does

Meaning being the grease of   the quasi-romantic   & the
military industrial

Flaneur or commentator   mordantly   over her   lush &
abundant

Translation is about   not   knowing

Neither   language

& then coming out

Where the notes do not fill them   we

Hold the following truths to be   true

When   words excite um   poets write   some

Friends

Partially

Government funded

334.2

The language of the tribe

Which gave us the word udder

Prowess at riding   the art of motorcycle maintenance

& portrayal of John Coltrane as Christ   among the lesser
saints

Animist tendencies towards electricity and children

Their humane & honorable relationship with AND songs of
strangling

All sexual relations with man & with nature

Fisted   at the onset of marriage—Laura—

All these things are now gone from The Vale

A mound of grass a castle a bottle of

The ghosts of standing   & the shadows & dreams

Buoy I proclaim—

In the life of a DJ (available for weddings and funerals Mon-
Sat)

Are all that remain

335

Tragedy is the mere commodification of suffering

Gabriel Gudding

because

you

are

a

fairy

and

have

no

bones

planes

no

longer

STOP

to go to the toilet

336

When I think of her which is often for her clothes are a little
tight

& remember that I am not & her hands up to the elbows
performing an oil change & I remember the dream of
the cream

which changes nipples back from brown to pink smearing it
& following her car

& I see her & hide all evidence of blogging from the living &
all food tastes

like books & I am scanning my elbows for posterity & living
with the attractiveness of

zen stepping into the river which is the same river & contains
the molecules

& the rudiments of Latin & if I make a chain & recycle with
zeal

& film myself with flaming creatures & honk if you practice
tantric sex

because this job description requires death in the sense that a
poem is death to public life & the sense that music
does not exist

except in the outer boroughs & planets & she whom I
imagined replies & sometimes

a receipt for having lived & I return to the catnip & the date

when the book says she left her clothes on 06.IV.1348   etc
    & amen

In a hair shirt & Rothmans   Mes amis!

As they inhibit me so shall I inhabit them

337

…& for endless afternoons Monday-Friday

I made a nest in the Tooting Working Men's Club Lounge
Bar Lounge

Learning that there is no such thing as an emergency

In the poetry world you touch something you don't know

& you say it feels like death for example & how

Books provide only moderate protection

If the best place to hide from meaning is in marriage

The world is so full of metaphor & generalization that it is
only possible to

blink at it

To live through lust is to live through sorrow & vice-versa

You have to have your head filled until it gets in the way

It feels like simile when the real world is always adjective

For how can we describe a frenzy of happiness

As the world moves from word to word to larger gestural
units

Then the options for oblivion become obvious

338

Because the big subjects need attention like a man (ha!)

Needs a maid Neil Young said because no filth   is intelligent
    enough

To change your life   & it is in the manner of horses
    hedgehogs & hippies

To hide beneath it   to grieve

The loss of a cup because it is old or a part off a body or a
    whole part

I brought back these presents

Or sock off

An extreme tool miracle

Saying   when will I stop writing this down

All the muck in   this life   when

The heart goes all out

& is

This real   Heaven

Charm naked & weak honey

339

Standing in Piccadilly Circus seeking satisfaction from a
large Chinese

When it was the 20th Century & impossible to imagine the
continuation of enlightenment or love

To a man from the 21st standing up besides being a writer &
saying in small volumes I am a writer

& it is imperative to do good things

In order to get things done an audience for poetry needs to
be famous

Because this project rarely rips the trousers

With all water heat & light running out of the designated
other

Horizontal & utopian in my nest

Her perfection filled the world & then heaven   meaning
perfect or dead

Which (imperative or question?)

Was the perfection of the imagination

In the bath on May evenings

Tossing all night beside the invisible wife

Saying I love you to a sonnet is really the best thing to say
because only it will listen

340

The secret of writing is to write

When fat—in a kaftan   or Hawaiian shirt when hirsute

Peering at love & the morning editorials

Because it is easier to be angry than confused

Dead people still feel happy on the Isle of Wight

Believing that when the workers own the means of
production they will fall asleep in the fields

& our bodies resonate together like onions

Then I am reminded of Phil Whalen

On his raspberry bed

How the dreams seep out

Mine sleep then disappear upon the eyelids of my daughter

Because of her golden ukulele

Only the shadows can make enough racket to keep me quiet

One day they will invent goggles so that we can see inside
one another

341

There is the suck & the suck & the suck

& the stink of the Thames at Woolwich

A box containing God Bless Tiny Tim

& her breasts reassembled on YouTube

It is a pleasure to recline on the deck & to cross it

Pulling off from complete thought & an attraction

The heart and the gargling art which was & no longer

Is still painful to me

Like insomnia wears off

A voice from a cloud on the cover

Makes the sun stand still

Like a little happiness in the eye nose or ear

She says   & yet

I only mentioned a syllable

342

In love with

Nothing

But

A memory like

A photo but

Only one

Light

Upon a

Bed

White

10 at night

Your long

Cool

Forearms

343

And the bolting or welding together of girders of steel to
form a cage

And the sky & the blue grey incandescence which pours out

And the glory of coffees viewed beneath fluorescent lights

And the cars and the cars and the cars men

And women who drive them & the glory of god in their
elbows & their knees

And feel comfortable on moss & increase human feeling

And lying horizontal or at a slight angle to the mind

Or the pleasures of marbles like the feeling of insomnia in the
chest

And then the beauty of constructivism & atonal music finally
arrives

Flooding the garden suburbs of South Croydon on Sundays

And the arrangement of molecules in the inconclusive

And the poor & the side-stapled ones

Wherever I have been in the universe

the leg   the life   the document

Fish only seen & the beauty of mercury

With two daughters   fresh food

Clean running water

The black skin which I have kissed

Pushing a screw into a haiku then filming it

Maybe dropping things or picking them up

Because in this life you never really

Own anything

In whatever package or format   on the jacket wrap   my hope
is to see & all

Planetary celebrators

As opposed to not

The ground that is under your feet

The Tottenham Court Road at times

Cracking it open & breathing it

Walking into a joke shop & finding language

Upon a package of novelty gum ones sometimes bleeding the
other one snapping

Dangerous slipping into the practice of universal compassion

Upon the subway back to Brooklyn

Midnight after a Harris Schiff reading

Actually having it being no different from thinking that you
have it

& then not wanting it

But not wanting it still being a position—like a cactus

Like these handcuffs

Marooned on a futon even a bad one from Ikea (footnote #31)

& the landfill & the outlook for Leos

Be wary of insects & cowboys

& remember the ending of history

In the playground

I have bigger fish to fry

Putting the arms back on

Fresh food

Clark Kenneth & William

Walking wiping reading weeding

With two daughters

0 & 7 /13 & 21 / 3 & 11

In a waterlogged flat

Singing   Gaily

O kids! O Books!

We love you!

Get up   & Get off!

Being happy with that

Feeling it daily

344

Making love in another man's
Autobiography   is always better   in real life
Worthy of a lover have I
Been loved   for what under   what light?
Orange constellations
Constellate   upon the
Orcadian   water
What does it mean   to be loved
On this Earth?
You have to ask
The coarser
Invective genres
¡Viva Zapatos!
Highlight the penetration

345 for & from Bernadette Mayer

Women are good

We live inside them

When ideas run out   more food in tins

Ones with fishes & the constant yearning

For the quick days in June thoughts of snow

In all part in point in singing part in the mountains

Instead of fucking you paint cracks on your feet

Men no longer step either on or in them

If I could invite myself to live with mathematicians

Cerebral from a stalagmitic presence

I don't have honey when you fuck me up the ass

In Piccadilly in seven snowsuits & no ticket

Look—My love is still a long way from heaven

Even Velasquez in Alaska would turn to other women

346

It is 13:47 & there are no demands to make love yet in this
    sonnet
The public school girls always wanted to fuck but you don't
    in heaven
Jamon Serrano & cheese calamari
Instead of fucking coffee & brandy is too hot
Or too cold there at the thigh tops there are no
Public school girls any more in this land
Sherry vinegar is interesting on peppers
Like water escapes from a guidebook or human
This is a big fat pencil which is interrupting
But not making love because you are dead
A key is a llave
I have not yet found it   it is
Now 13:58 the only place where my hand rests is
At the end of my wrist   & love   you cannot have it

347

Concerning the possibility of communication
Between the living & the dead
As sign lovers
In sign language
Poked at with a stick & shouted at in Vietnamese
Woken up from maple-syrup-induced delirium
& the need to write it
Going a very long way with a little Edith Piaf
True in the real world & not just in books
If being married to an idea is the same or different to being
married
Is it possible to learn to love the world so much
That it loves us back
Thinking not thinking on futon or carpet
Grown weary of sexually suggestive dancing

348

Which is soothed but not satiated by cowboy songs

The Yellow Rose Of Texas is one

Which is not cured by hanging an arm or a leg over the side
of the paint stops

Burning where books are outthrust   which in this current
woman is long

Like Michael Jackson

In search of the Nobel Prize for Literature

Which I don't have just yet

Fluttering like drums

Which makes me at 4AM just or quite

Beautiful in the numbers of teeth

Which I still have here

Let me show them

Beautiful

Going like a small planet to a large planet

349

Smoke signals signal smoke only to cowboys

Or geisha who can't read them   waiting for a wave of the hankie or code poem from the nubile & dead ones

Who never come   to Alamo Road London SW19   there is an eternal pointlessness to the counting of hormones

A joke something about a horse in a bar

Of ambiguous sexuality or stamp   balm to a   bus full of cowboy poets

Hopelessness or moral stance   so vague that I hardly recognize myself

Soaring through bright skies with bright eyes

So high that I might see my true love

Happy to live on a diet of bird seed and scratch cards

Pretending to be Burt Lancaster or Charlton Heston at the organ

Or soft & untroubled   like a carpet   I have sent off my check

Waiting for these $3.99 X Ray Spex   to get closer to the "poetry" of sex

Saved & inflamed by the prospect of death

But not there yet

350

I have been awaiting if you have not noticed   since poem
338 a visitation

Ovid said Forma bonum fragile est & did mean it & I said
Questo nostro caduco et fragile bene

Really   fragile & perishable indeed   like the guru in the
beard & gold Rolls Royce said to his 400 women

In the mountains   because they alone knew him   concerning
the fates and the winds   & beauty which was so like a
city   & like an invisible city   remained
hidden

In my life teaching English to 2394 people but

What else could I do?

Nothing   On   Earth   Without   Love   my   language
sucked it all up & then spat me back out

First meaning and then nothingness   in the right or
wrong order

I mean—

Darling do this to me

It being important to see & feel everything   Beard Guy said
"Never died

Never born"

Looked in the mirror & then finally

Knackered & cosmopolitan   for the pleasure of a glimpse of
    it

I   believed   him

351

My speech was mottled with the dusky dawns and I stormed the spot on a cow

Clark Coolidge

Meanness in atriums and cog realms

No longer sticks to an insect consumed by divine love

Able to look into the lens & be

Like to a nightingale shrouded in casements

With the pretence that every temper leans towards agates

So divine that it brings man felicity or ferocity & a saint book
    with lids

& so justify the life   quick through the numbers

The notion of the Pythagorean letter Y is not entirely stupid

A copy of the universe is one thing too many in the face of
    salvation

Goading extant   to work   rootless   from Morden to
    Melancholia not Mine

On the road from childhood to adultery

Within every chromosome & still sick

These are not mine

Shrill leaks from composition

352

Sweating over   the next big thing

My book   my imaginary

Lover   Whose eyes

I like to rub

That shone more brightly than the sun

Size sounds in my memory

On fire with a virtuous thought

A cat no longer strapped   in an Amen Corner surgery

To have her gonads torn off

When you left this world so did love

Only to become   later in the story

More like an angel than a lady

Unfolding & taut

Face smeared & flared tail folding

353

……………………………………..……singing….

……………………………….……………time passing

………….the night……………………………………

…………………………………...………………month

…………………………..……………………………

…………………………………….…….my……..

…………………………….……………this….

………………………….painful……………

……………………………………………….

that…………………………………..….life

………….which to me Death & Heaven seem mean

…….the season & the hour………………

………………..sweet years………….

To speak…… .with piety my invitation

353.3 for & from Musa & Durling

Wandering bird that go   O lovely little bird   Singing
    away   Singing or else

Weeping for past time   in tones of grief
    for all the time gone by   for past time

Seeing night and winter   you see the night and winter
    before you at your side

The day   and day   and the happy
    months behind   and all those happy months
    behind

Aware as you are if as you know   of your grievous
    troubles   your own grievous troubles

You also knew   could you be so   of my
    plight as your own   my similar state

You would come you would fly   straight to the bosom
    of this wretch   to my unconsoled bosom

To share its sorrowing groans   to share with him
    some of his painful grief

I do not know if   I cannot say   our
    portions would be equal   our portions would
    be equal

Since she you weep for   for she whom you weep for
    may still have her life is perhaps still in life

With which Heaven and Death of which Death and Heaven
are for me are stingy so stingy to me

But the forbidding season but the forbidding season
and hour and the hour

The memory of sweet years invite me with the memory
and bitter ones of the sweet and bitter ones

Invites me to discuss to speak to you with you
my pity with pity

She who you for she whom you perhaps
still in life may still have

354

In the joke about Petrarch the naked man is

Love & my fragile

A man lives to complain along the lines of the work

To do the job of the living fish and dog things

& of beings alive in a camera ascending & no longer truculent able finally to care for a cactus to avoid seeing

As a responsible act talking because what else removes the pleasure

From the realms of poet or pirate death

The need to be immortal vs. the way that some roads are

More useful than what befalls the translator who lives alone

The limits of my language are the limits of my income

The limits of my income are the limits of my world

The limits of my language are the limits of my—Laura

No thought quite large enough to fill in this hole

The light shoots right through me when I lie on the nail

355

On Hampstead Heath at the bathing pools

Toxicity or glue shirt across the city for the purpose of being
touched & but

Of its swiftness through the sump & the sex

Unable to encounter young mothers

At full moon parties my eyes went from the wet ones of an
ostrich & lashes to the brick-like

Limed things   bombed out   from downloading

The heat trapped in screens & released by relaxation

The best way to be cured of love is to sleep with a cactus

The slickest tools' course when the soul departs from the
ams

The big hand still moves faster than the little hand

It is always a hard shirt art or swan body to fill with love

On Hampstead Heath at the bathing pools

Dressed as Keats   in summer & thus anonymous

Rimmed with   kohl & recent purchase

356

Infatuated with sleep the sacred law   inhales me   comedic
(not)   & (unwillingly) quasi-celibate

In a clip joint   that spanned two centuries   inebriated with &
to   the pursuit of fame & obsessive with writing habit

To eternity   any method or neck suggests itself   in search
of love

Which I could not do to her living   for lack of human
interest or oriental tap

Like the premonition of sudden death indicates   a sudden
ache in the ball & the longing for support or
physicians

But my woman's a man & her bone   blows man's blood
cold

To her psychiatry = one boot of cement which is   for
suckers & the other of self-pity & sin

She goes into the world avoiding the underwear in shops
selling underwear   because it's for women

Once again on the Left Bank   in Peckham   I put on a
suit made of aspirin

Remembering how it was possible for a woman to make a
man happy

With only small animals   butter   cucumbers & a loaf of
bread & then

Out   of romantic love   assume all marital habits

Little knowing (as they say) there was only   domesticity at
the end of the rainbow

& less than 2 hours life left in the rabbit

357

Every day seems like 1000 years to me

The years of a lifetime are a flash of lightning; who clings to objects? They are empty through and through.

Until I can follow her where she's (dead) gone

Ultimately, what is what?

Who I ran after in this world & who guided me

In this life, purity

Unconstrained by the lies

I would say I am within, making offerings to billions of Buddhas

Of this world because I now know them & so much light

The Way. Why? Simply

Inside my heart sent from Heaven that

Ultimately, how is it? [Silence]

I began to count up my time and my losses

What is the principle behind "what thing is it that comes?" [Silence]

Nor do I fear the threats of death

This is my whisk; what is the scripture?

When Jesus suffered many worse pains

I have a statement.

To enable me to follow him

In the flow of birth and death; even imparting

Having recently entered every one of her veins

"You don't really understand"

She—who was my destiny

Finding nothing that was not medicine

May now reach the end of me

Without turning away from the multitudes of people, body
    and mind drop off

& no marks appear to cloud   her clear face   whose destiny
    was (or was not)   to love me

Try further to explain that principle

358

& so I slept with thespians

Cucumbers apples and pears

By drawing a circle & placing myself at the centre

Because I did not like it much

If warm & naked on a lake   in a pink shirt

Pressing neck to neck to neck

All selfless love & hope of the metaphor called heaven

Which for you means the extinguishing of it

Self-harm obligations   & menthol tabs

When the teeth meet the cheek

& the sun & the stars & the moon list

A lover loves—for all that

In spite of a phenomenology of spirit

When a cat gets cancer the vet kills the cat

359

I ask my eye to do things   like fall on the whiteness of milk
  or   the red rubber bands on the pavement

but my eye says no   my eye says you have seen enough &
  wasted it   & it was enough   being soft

until the things that were forced in or upon upset me like the
  children   just lying there   in the war book with no
  feet hands or elbows

while you read   this world is   decomposition   as
  explanation when I wanted pink melon joy & you did
  not listen

to the heart when it was revolted or the ankle or the neck   in
  the picture   with this example

being cowardly in IKEA when you sought her heart through
  invention but

could not find it   or life in South London   tired by subtitles
  and your border   translation

of hysteria into an addiction to service industries and
  shopping the eye says you gave up early on love

but replaced it with nothing my eye says you look to writing
  but are found wanting

my eye says look at your life but she will not let you it says
  you suffer because you thought

you had two but now you have only one food is all that is left
    you

you better speak to your tongue

if it will still let you you ask your eye to do things   your eye
    will not listen because now that we're done

the sky will no longer let you

360

This is my Tokyo Hot Sonnet

Bending the M-Leg

In the car that makes the ostium

Alternately sucking the close-up scene

The car & fourth cock

After math by intense finger

The distant star

With backflow genius

From which the cloud semen was poured

A masterpiece necessary to give up the leg

The missionary posture totals

The fur light

Gathered at bending piston

The distant star ejaculates on the sofa

After the you is licked & the nipple

Dynamite & milks at bending

Totals deeply at mission

At the scene of the r

Pourings & deep kiss

That understand what is happening

& Y man's groin cloudiness

Car & carpet endurance at entrance

A cloud of intestine juice foolishness

Dynamite & the open-leg pose

The state joy enhanced by seeming

Completely missionary finger

Raked out of Rod McKuen

Getting high & watching television

Whose star is a cowboy wandering

Robbed of all ambition

360.2 I am Francis Petrarch

I

Had summit

Flames fear and begin which I suffered

Patience overcome then cruel a flatterer can unhappiness

Complaints

Against much

False amorous peace and one care I he's

Sharpening desire with cruel a wretch why

High

And me

For hair obstinate cannot accuse bitter sweet

Rapacious thieves thorny barbarous and hardships cares here

I've

Any my

Force lord has sounded which this parts

Practiced the art words rather nor complain who

Desire

That harm

Life misery and risen could risen its

Speaking gave softness her that survive presence these

Thinks

Are my

Far greater than women such ingrate such

Appealing raised that there among are collect his

In

Places might

Famous learned and one service I thousand

Pleasure vile youngster her a impression criticizes ghosts

Is toward man

Fly through mortal things could risen first

Pitched voice sentence pleasure have heard such

II.

Having

Part summit

Refined fire make plaint justice I his

Patience mine hated suffering and virtuous cruel what

Wit

Has my

Life amorous

361

Flared to parsing   beyond the vegetable close-ups

On a mattress of star spattered plaster

Clasping the collected stories of the Fu Manchu

Headcharged yet wormless

Waiting to hatch coils   panels of overlapping & dwarf
crocuses   in a ginger syrup

To cover a bald patch worn by rubbing it on floors with
imaginary paper   dwarves or elves

Poofter's froth & Campari   bright hay   propane tax
"hemorrhoid-sublime" star puffs

I see clearly now how our lives fly by & The Movement

I see Oh! Inside Alice Coltrane

& I see Oh! Inside www.intercourse.com & it is dull

I remember when   I could break loose   like—

A cat in this life   but no longer

Whose hair balls repulsed only

Less adventurous women

362

then

a

voice

says

now

that

I'm

dead

it

is

possible

to

love

you

363

This is the Buddha life indeed
Breathing or otherwise
Although until now
  I could not have named it
Whatever light
There is to lie in
  Mind decides it
The human condition
Is often not sweet
Having no Buddha-nature
  & no I to find it
This is the Buddha life indeed
Alive who has tried it
All existence entwined
  I   is   empty   inside it

364

Oh money I loved you   but not really gone beyond it

Tabasco sauce & keys motorway bridges & their   powder
grey   concrete tops dropped into bracketed gaps across
the tracks

Indian fud & sorbets   attachment to what all lack

Dressing up   like a bearded lady & back   in line #
something to the propinquities of soon being dead   &
father no longer   a Buddhist of sorts

Map reading which pleased the eye on the ring roads round
Paris

Camping in the Glastonbury mud   reading Walt texting
mumps from this distance & timber

Even though I would not like to hear The Moody Blues one
more time singing

Written never meaning   whistling oh don't you cry for me I
come from Barcelona   with my daughters

On my knees   looking up at the swallows   while I was
thinking hard about everything   & vice-versa

Mustering the energy to sit   I am dreaming now of being a
fish

Something   & my answer come to this   gone beyond it

When you take a fish out of water   Satori—is—no longer a
        fish   the way

To write with some insight   about life

Is to idle   & avoid all temptation

364.2

At last! At last! All of reality! We find we are

what we only pretended to be.

Robert Duncan

3 x Cucumber

65 x Fuck

25 x Daughter

49 x Leg

24 x London

46 x Death

10 x Shopping

6 x Marx

10 x Buddha

60 x Sex

93 x Poetry/Poet

4 x Jeff

399 x Lover / love

18 x & yet / and yet

365

How lovely to be King of the Beats

With a big hard dawn   on Oxford Street

Moving among men moths & the beauty of stepping on
        cracks   with impunity

Because today I wrote nothing & am

Only an ugly man   & the same thing tomorrow

Reft in rehab   away   with the raggle-taggle gypsies O

Myopic   gargantuan   & self-loathing   in tights

Gargling love-struck & doom 366 times   in one lifetime
        Laura finally

In a bucky pelt   you are the only hope that I have

In Sonnet #98   Shakespeare will copy dead me
        unacknowledgedly   who

For a moment thought   I   was he—

The King of the Beats   in a dream   when really

I was just   King of the Swedes

& the only Empress is the Empress of Ice-Cream

366

The boys are singing to drive away the noxious birds

Before women it is useful to practice on statues

& now I am here to tell you all that I have discovered

That living is one of the best things—there where I ripped it

That her eyes couldn't have been more beautiful—I just
    thought they were

Driving my utopian car over the dystopian roads

I go over and look at myself

& look surprised

Because living is one of the best things   I go over

I stand there listening to the sunshine burning the grass

My horn a crumpled dream

Earthlings! Comrades! ¡Adiós!

Work out your salvation with diligence

As if all things were still possible

These poems have appeared in earlier versions in the following books and publications:

Petrarch (Crater) With thanks to R.T.A Parker (huge thanks)

Pet Soundz (Crater)

Petrarch (Barque Press) With thanks (& apologies & love) to Andrea Brady & Keston Sutherland

Petrarch (Book Thug) With thanks to Jay MillAr, Steve Collis, & Amy De'Ath

The Reality Street Book of Sonnets (Reality Street) With thanks to Jeff Hilson

Gaspar Orozco's translations are forthcoming in an anthology—*Enemigos* (pub. Mexico City)

Magazines: *The Sienese Shredder, Blackbox Manifold, High Zero, Vanitas, The Other Room, Delirious Hem, How2*. Many thanks to all of the editors. I do apologize if I have forgotten anyone.

The Poets' Home Companion template came via Larry Fagin & Miles Champion.

With thanks to Laird Hunt, Jèssica Pujol i Duran, David Kelly-Mancaux, Kent Johnson, Amy De'Ath, Eleni Sikelianos, Jeff Hilson, Lisa Jarnot, Michael Gizzi, Peter Jaeger, S.J. Fowler, John Latta / & to Clark Coolidge—the brightest mine & the beatest richardsnary.

And to the several hundred poets whose words run through these pages.

Always everything for Koto Daisy & Yuki Lily

CRATER 27

JUNE 2014

ISSN 0948 2041

LONDON

www.ingramcontent.com/pod-product-compliance
Lightning Source LLC
Chambersburg PA
CBHW051802230426
43672CB00012B/2595
* 9 7 8 1 9 0 7 5 7 0 5 0 6 *